Love and MONEY

Other Books by Sylvia Porter

Sylvia Porter's Money Book
Sylvia Porter's New Money Book for the 80's
Sylvia Porter's Annual Tax Book
Sylvia Porter's Your Own Money

Love and MONEY

by SYLVIA PORTER

with the Contributors to
Sylvia Porter's Personal Finance Magazine

William Morrow and Company, Inc. / New York

Library of Congress Cataloging in Publication Data

Porter, Sylvia Field, 1913–
    Love and money.

    Includes index.
    1. Finance, Personal. 2. Marriage. 3. Home
economics—Accounting. I. Sylvia Porter's personal
finance magazine. II. Title.
HG179.P565   1985   332.024   85-11536
ISBN 0-688-06056-0

Printed in the United States of America

First Edition

1 2 3 4 5 6 7 8 9 10

BOOK DESIGN BY RICHARD ORIOLO

Contents

ACKNOWLEDGMENTS

We wish to express our appreciation and gratitude to the following authors who allowed us to include or to quote from the articles listed below. Most of the articles originally appeared in *Sylvia Porter's Personal Finance Magazine*:

Jean Baer for *The Art of Sticking to a Budget* and *The Actual and Hidden Cost of Getting a Divorce*. Nella G. Barkley for *Money Talk Makes Good Pillow Talk*. Michelle Bekey for *Choosing the Right Checking Account*. Charlotte Crenson for *Divorce and Social Security, Social Security Questions and Answers,* and *You Don't Have To Be Old To Love Social Security*. Eleanor Dienstag for *Budget Makeover: Pamela Wood and Bruce Kirch* and *When She Earns More Than He*. Claudia Flisi for *Overlapping Employee Benefits* and *The Cost of a Mistress or a Young Male Lover*. Morris Gold for *Taxes and Your Work*. Janis Graham for *Budget Makeover: Meet the Jacksons, Credit: Yours, Mine,* and *Ours*, and *The Two-Career Dilemma*. Tim Harper for *Prenuptial Agreements*. Annie Moldafsky for *Budget Makeover: Lisa Robinson and Kim Treviranus*. Dana Shilling for *All in the Family Business*. George Spelvin for *Of Wills and Probate*. Catherine Stribling for *How Creditors Keep Track of Your Paying Habits*. Ciji Ware for *Budget Makeover: Meet the Moores* and *Budget Makeover: Struggling Entrepreneurs*. Sidney Weinman for *Combining Business and Pleasure, Taxes and Your Family, In Whose Name Should You Own Assets?*, and *Divorce and Taxes*.

With special thanks to the following members of the *SPPFM* editorial staff: Patricia Schiff Estess, editor; Elana Lore, executive editor; Arthur H. Rogoff, managing editor; Ellen Goldschmidt, associate editor; Katharine L. Ramsden, research editor; Ellen Hermanson, contributing editor; and Jeanette McClain, editorial assistant. And with very special thanks to Nellie Sabin, outside editor on this project. Particularly my gratitude to Walter Meade, who was the inspiration for this book and its title, *Love and Money*.

INTRODUCTION

et's face it: If you're romantically involved, you're financially involved. Love and money may be the most vital parts of your life, and they are more closely entwined than you may think.

In this book, we are digging deep into fundamentals—into the finances of relationships—and here we have truly moved into uncharted areas. Whatever your situation, you'll find essential information here to guide you through the problems, pitfalls, and rewards of managing your financial affairs along with your affairs of the heart.

Should you sign a prenuptial agreement to protect your property? If your partner is transferred, should you follow? How should you handle the finances of living together? As a mistress, what kind of reimbursement can you expect? Do you thoroughly realize the explosive potentials when a wife earns more than her husband and the strategies for eliminating those potentials? Are you and your partner financially compatible? Do you know how to make a working relationship with your spouse pay off in tax savings? What should you go after in a divorce settlement?

I hope the knowledge you will gain from these answers will help you in the most important relationships of all: the relationships of your own life. Read, enjoy—and win!

One MONEY TALK MAKES GOOD PILLOW TALK

ou feel things have been quite edgy at home for some time now. You don't really know why. You both have good jobs. He could be considered on the "fast track" in a substantial, well-respected firm. Your position as a paralegal is very satisfying. Every time you suggest going out for dinner or buying a new dress, he tells you how extravagant you are. You can't put your finger on what's the matter, because it seems to you there is enough coming in to enjoy life a bit. You maintain a joint checking account, but recently he acts as though he wants to be the only one to write the checks.

What has happened here is not unusual. The people involved have neglected to communicate with one another. He, she, or both have made significant assumptions, either about what the other person wants or about the "right" way for the two of them to spend money, and they failed to check out these assumptions.

The problem is broader than lack of communication about money, though, for how you want to spend your money is intimately connected with how you want to spend your life.

The situation above is troubling because money does not appear to be a concern, but the husband seems very edgy about every dollar being spent. Probably every couple has felt some symptoms of this disparity in attitude at one time or another.

Putting yourself in the woman's place in this situation, you are confused. You don't know what exactly is wrong or when it started being that way. You wonder if you are imagining the whole thing.

Left to your own devices, you would be enjoying life. Although you wouldn't admit it to anyone, you know you've thought more than once recently about what it would be like to be living alone again, supporting yourself on your paralegal's salary and being independent of what is feeling more and more like a hassle. Of course, you wouldn't actually be alone. There are the children to consider. Anyway, such an idea is unthinkable, but you wonder where all of the fun of life has gone.

Meanwhile, without your knowing it, your husband is seething. He views your behavior as totally irresponsible. Just at the time when you need to be planning for your future, your children's future, setting money aside for some wise investments, you appear only to be interested in what movie to go to on Saturday night.

To make matters worse, for him and for you, you seem to have absolutely no ambition in your job. You're clearly good enough to go on to law school and make that important next step up. The kids are old enough to manage on their own a bit. He feels that putting you through law school would be a sensible investment, despite the fact that he feels under tremendous pressure.

He knows that his next fifteen years in the business will go even faster than the last fifteen, and he has been feeling isolated with the burden of having to do all the thinking and planning for family and retirement by himself.

What could have been done along the way to prevent this situation?

- From the onset of your relationship, have planning review sessions—at least annually—serious ones lasting a day.
- Talk about who will be the principal breadwinner at what points in your lives and why. Make mutual decisions.
- Attempt to recognize the personal monetary and psychological costs of each decision. Actually write them down on a legal pad, one sheet for him and one for her. They could look like this:

The Principal Breadwinner

PLUSES	MINUSES
1) power	1) burden
2) control	2) absolute time commitment to job

The Contributing Breadwinner

PLUSES	MINUSES
1) more flexibility in time and choice of career	1) less ability to influence financial choices
2) low stress	2) possible loss of credibility in spouse's eyes

- Each of you write down what you want out of life and then show it to the other.
- Each of you write down what is fun for you and show it to the other.
- Draw up budgets together so that you each have the same information.
- Include each other's "fun" items in your budgets.

What can be done now?

Don't lose a week's time. Act immediately, because the situation could get out of control. Set aside a day when you can arrange to have the kids away and take a long drive to some pleasant spot (maybe have a picnic) and talk. Say that you know things haven't been going well lately and acknowledge discomfort on each of your parts. If your partner won't own up to this discomfort, then insist, at the least, that yours has to be dealt with and that you are willing to do your part. Write down what you are willing to do, commit to do, and do it. What you write down and give to him might look something like this:

1) I will plan each Wednesday evening to fix a gourmet, candlelit dinner, and we will talk about whatever you (or I) wish.

2) I will research financial planning courses and make a decision, within a month, as to which one to enroll in, so I can learn more about the whole subject.

Explain why you don't see yourself going to law school, but do so against a backdrop of what you *can* do to make things easier for him and for the family.

If this doesn't encourage both of you to open up and commit to the same process, suggest outside professional assistance before you're in an irreversible downward spiral.

Often disagreements about how much money will be spent, accumulated, or planned for are simply signals that something else is out of sync. That's not to say that an ample supply of money doesn't smooth things out a bit, but a bit is about all. The wealthy couple certainly doesn't display any long-term immunity from interpersonal conflict.

At the real heart of this story is a failure to share some incredibly important information:

- what your feelings about money are;
- what material things are important to you;
- what you want to do with your time;

- what's fun to you;
- what your fascinations are;
- what you don't like;
- what your daily financial needs are (the things you can't function without);
- what your goals are—financial and others.

And, usually accompanying this failure to share or talk about what's going on inside your head is a failure to listen adequately to or observe what's going on with the other person.

Communication works both ways and definitely happens by looking and listening as well as talking. When the process is working well, both partners are constantly sending and receiving valuable information, which helps them spend their money and their time appropriately for both of them.

If the paralegal wife had more information from her husband, she could help him alleviate some of his stress. On the other hand, she has probably never taken much of a look at what she wanted to do with her life. Apparently an easygoing, fun-loving, and not professionally ambitious woman, she had unconsciously placed the "family security" burdens on her husband while seeming to contribute by virtue of her job. If she could have put some of her feelings into words, he would not have placed so much unspoken blame on her for not taking the steps to become a lawyer. At the very least, they would have known more of what they were dealing with.

The key question is "What do I want to accomplish with my life?"

It takes time, discipline, and the right environment to reach the answer to that question, but actually, you can have a good time approaching it from its many angles.

Whatever little insights you can get into the things you want, share them and invite your spouse to do the same. Beware of the danger signals that flag problems: silence, secretiveness, or sudden outburst.

The price of not communicating is to proceed to the point where differences appear irreconcilable. Even seemingly irreconcilable differences, though, are subject to compromise when the factors which underlie them are aired.

Pillow talk makes good dollars and sense. It's your investment in a long-term relationship.

MINGLING
SINGLES

 f you're single—at whatever age, for whatever reason—you have special financial considerations that are not the same as those for people who are living together (see Chapter 3) or married (see Chapter 5). Chances are you are part of the dating scene, which brings with it certain dilemmas. Or it's possible that you are a mistress or lover being supported by someone else. Whatever your single situation happens to be, money will play a part in your relationships. If you approach the financial side of your more intimate connections with as much creativity as you, say, prepare *saumon en croute* or redecorate your living room, the results could surprise you.

DATING

Dating doesn't *have* to cost a bundle—but it often does. The big issue here is: who pays? If you are the kind of gentleman who insists on footing every bill, your getting around may end up putting you behind. And if you are the kind of lady who thinks that purses are only for perfume, think again. These days, both sexes know how to earn a dollar as well as how to spend it, and equality—or sharing, if you prefer—is the name of the game.

If you are a woman who isn't comfortable having your date pick up every tab, there are ladylike ways of paying your own way even if your date doesn't like it when you offer to do so. First of all, don't "volunteer" to pay. Instead, why don't *you* make the dinner reservations next time? That way, you can request on the phone that the check be given to you. Confirm that arrangement when you get to the restaurant. And if the waiter forgets and places the check in front of your escort, reach over, take it, smile, and say, "I'll get it."

You can also "arrange" to get to the ticket window first at the movie theater so you can buy two tickets. If you and your date plan to go to dinner and a show, suggest that he take care of one and you'll pay for the other. Use a friendly tone and manner, but make it clear that there is only one polite reply.

The point is to take action. Don't wait for your date to suggest that you pay or to approve your idea.

There may be some men who refuse ever to let you pay for a single activity, but I'll bet that most will be pleased—and maybe relieved—to share the expense of dating.

MAINTAINING A MISTRESS OR A MALE LOVER

If you'd like to keep a mistress or a male lover, the most important thing to bear in mind is that it can be very expensive.

If you'd like to *be* a mistress or a male lover, the fundamental thing to remember is the extent of your rights in this capacity:

For the most part, you don't have any. However, you do have financial options you may not be aware of.

But that is not to say that being kept is necessarily a bad deal. Take the case of two female friends from New York who met men when they were both in their twenties. One woman married her lover; the other could not because he was already married. But he set her up in a Manhattan apartment, which he bought in her name.

A decade later, both relationships had ended. And the divorcée moaned to her friend, "After eight years of marriage, I got a sofa and some dishes. But you got equity."

Definitions

Before you can talk about the cost of keeping a mistress or male lover, terms have to be defined. Is a mistress anyone from a regular hooker to a common-law wife? Is she always kept by a married man? Is a male lover invariably a gigolo (taken from the French word *gigolette*, or prostitute)? Is the male lover always younger than the woman who keeps him? What does it mean to be "kept" these days, when the majority of women are in the work force?

For purposes of this discussion, a mistress is neither a prostitute (one who provides sexual favors strictly for money) nor a common-law wife (who gives all outward appearances—as does her partner—of being in a conventionally married situation). A mistress is someone involved with a man in an unlawful relationship that includes sex and is of some duration.

Unlawful requires further explanation. A few states still have outdated laws prohibiting fornication between consenting adults who are not married to each other. But that is more a legal oddity than a basis for criminal action. Adultery has been decriminalized, and in at least forty-five states today, it is no longer grounds for divorce.

The "sex" aspect also needs elaboration. If sex were the sole basis for the relationship, mistresses would have no legal standing. They wouldn't be able to lay claim to estates after their lovers died or seek compensation if their lovers had a change of heart after many years of togetherness. Financial compensation for sexual services is considered to be "against public policy" by the courts.

But if a relationship can be demonstrated on a nonsexual basis, a mistress improves her legal standing. Marvin Mitchelson, the lawyer who squired the famous Lee Marvin "palimony" case through the California courts in 1976, is currently arguing cases of this kind in California and New York.

Some duration is a flexible term calling for a little common sense. There's no average length of time for a lovers' relationship, just as there isn't for marriage. Some go on for decades; others fade out after a few months or years. The longer-lasting the love affair, the greater the expectation that there will be compensation for the value of the companionship provided.

A mistress, as we define it, is not just any woman involved in a long-term love affair. She may be by some definitions, but we are using the term to refer to a kept woman, one who is supported largely, if not entirely, by a man. That's not so common in this day and age.

What is somewhat common about mistresses is that they are usually—although not always—kept by married men. And the men are usually older, the women younger. Because this arrangement seems to be so much more prevalent than that of the older woman supporting a younger man (for all the same complex variegated reasons), we'll talk a lot more about mistresses here.

Does being "kept" imply sexual fidelity as well as financial support? One banker put it this way, "I expect a hell of a lot more sexual fidelity if I pay all the bills than if I pay some of them." An understanding about fidelity seems to be implied in many cases, especially where the mistress sees her lover on a regular basis.

In one situation, a married man brings his mistress to Florida along with his wife and children. The mistress is ensconced in a separate apartment, discreetly distant from the rest of the family, but she is visited regularly by her lover.

Talking Basic Costs: The Ultra-Rich

The median income for a young woman age 24–35 in the United States today is $15,082. For a male in the same age bracket, it is $20,584. So according to these figures it doesn't really cost a lot to set someone up with a better-than-median income.

However, this median income is not necessarily the yearly cost of keeping a lover. The price tag for a moderately stylish setup in Manhattan might run $50,000 for starters. In San Francisco it might be a little less—say, $30,000. In Beverly Hills you'd have to add in the cost of the de rigueur Mercedes.

Add a certain allowance for hairdressers and stylish clothing and a piece of jewelry for Christmas, and the costs begin to mount. If the mistress isn't working at all, she needs some sort of health insurance plan or membership in a Health Maintenance Organization.

But all of this should not present a problem to the very wealthy men who are supporting mistresses. A man worth several million dollars need not concern himself with a hundred thousand here or there.

Tax Considerations for the Wealthy

The primary tax repercussion of compensating one's lover with straight cash gifts is that you run afoul of the IRS. If you give an individual more than $10,000 in one year, says the Internal Revenue Service, you have to fill out a gift tax form. But this rule is difficult to enforce and, according to a number of lawyers, it is observed as much in the breach as in the practice.

A wealthy man might prefer the possibility of an IRS violation to the certainty of his wife's displeasure. And a wife is often advised not to blow the whistle to the IRS. If she does, then files for divorce and support, she has diminished her husband's estate by the amount of fraud uncovered and risked the chance he might go to jail, leaving her without a steady source of alimony payments.

Tax Considerations for the Rest of Us

What if you want to maintain a mistress and you're not an ultra-millionaire? In other words, you're in love but you're not in oil, and some tax advantages would be nice. There are a number of ways people have approached this. Some of these may be disallowed by the IRS and create the possibility for criminal prosecution:

Direct Compensation

- Getting your mistress a job in your company, where she may or may not be expected to work. This is particularly advantageous if the company is yours. For example, in New York, when a man hires a secretary to work for him at $20,000 a year, the after-tax cost to him will be only about $8,500. In addition, there is a side benefit: should the wife find out about the mistress and sue for divorce, the man's income is $20,000 less than would otherwise have appeared in his records.
- Getting your mistress a job where you work. In Washington, D.C., where government jobs—at less than a millionaire's salary—are many, mistresses frequently wind up on someone's payroll. The job is helpful not only for the straight salary but also for the medical and life insurance benefits a government official might be hard pressed to subsidize out of his own pocket.
- Setting her up as an officer in a dummy corporation.
- Encouraging her to earn a real estate broker's license and using that as a conduit for compensation.
- Investing in a business she has started, or giving her seed money to get one going.

Lodging

- Renting or buying her an apartment as an office for your company.
- Buying her a house or apartment as an investment property.

Long-term compensation

- Giving her non-voting stock in a family-owned business.
- Setting up a Totten Trust. You, as originator of the trust, can draw upon it during your lifetime, and the remainder goes to the designated beneficiary after you die. The trust becomes part of your taxable estate but not your probate estate. Other kinds of trust arrangements may also be explored.

Incidentals

- Items such as cars, dinners, entertainment, and travel can be and often are tucked under the umbrella of "business expenses."
- Clothing presents more of a problem if you are looking for a tax break. If your paramour is an aspiring actress, not a secretary, it's a lot easier to handle that $300 negligee or the $1,000 Armani suit. The $50,000 Fendi fur might still be hard to explain to the IRS.

Life Insurance

What happens when the supporting partner dies? Let's take the case of a fifty-year-old man and his mistress, who is twenty years younger. He promises to provide for her after his death but doesn't want his wife to find out, so he can't include his mistress in his will. What are his options?

In addition to cash gifts, stocks and bonds, and investment-grade collectibles (jewelry, art, furs) during the course of their affair, he might want to take out an insurance policy on his life. But there are obstacles, the most significant of which is the insurance company's question about the proposed beneficiary: Does she have an "insurable interest" in the insured party?

Here a single man has a definite advantage over his married, mistress-keeping counterpart. Most insurance companies today will conduct an investigation on the purchase of any life policy with a face value exceeding $150,000–$200,000. A single woman who is keeping company with a single man, regardless of the exact circumstances of their relationship, can usually demonstrate "insurable interest."

But a married man who is keeping company with any other woman spells the kind of trouble insurers want to stay away from. For one thing, the moral aspects of such a situation are anathema to the conservative, upstanding image insurance companies try to maintain.

Then there's the more practical side. If the wife found out, might she not be so outraged as to pull the trigger on her philandering spouse? And might the insurance company not then be compelled to pay up to the grieving mistress? A poor insurance risk all the way around.

Let's say, however, that a wealthy man can find an accommodating insurance agent. Should he buy the policy in his own name or hers? And should he buy term or universal/whole life insurance?

If he buys insurance and names his mistress as beneficiary, it becomes part of his taxable—although not probated—estate. So the wife finds out. Also, he can change the designated beneficiary at any time. There is no guarantee of support to the mistress unless he names her an irrevocable beneficiary.

Term insurance presents an additional complication. Is the policy paid up for one year, for five years, or up to the moment the man dies, whenever that may be? In the former cases, the mistress again has no real security. In the latter case, the cost would be so prohibitive, compared to other long-term investments, as to be ludicrous.

A wiser alternative is to create an irrevocable trust into which the man would pay up to $10,000 a year (abiding by IRS gift-tax guidelines) for the purchase of a universal or whole-life policy. A fifty-year-old man could purchase a policy with a $5-million face value on that basis. If he paid into it for at least three years, the mistress would be able to collect the full amount upon his death. And the yearly payments would never exceed $10,000, no matter how long the man lived.

Best of all, the trust arrangement would remove this policy from the man's estate . . . and keep it his private affair even after his death.

Cohabitation Agreements

Depending on your point of view, cohabitation agreements are either the greatest thing since goat cheese or the source of untold grief for many a romance. (For more on living together, see Chapter 3.)

In theory, cohabitation agreements are a great boon to a mistress, whose legal rights are otherwise arguable. Such agreements are recognized as binding contracts on the presumption that the time two people spend together is valuable.

The Mitchelson/Marvin "palimony" case established a precedent: the legal recognition of the non-sexual contribution of a mistress to a relationship. The argument turns on the validity of an oral or implied contract, much more difficult to prove in court than a written document.

Unlike prenuptial contracts, cohabitation agreements do not provide for a division of assets in case of termination of the relationship. But they should assure the mistress of something in case the relationship ends abruptly and without warning—continuing maintenance of a separate apartment in her name, for example.

The basic problem with cohabitation agreements is that most people don't like them very much. A man who may be willing to promise the moon during the throes of passion finds his ardor cooling quickly when his words are being nailed down in black and white. While cohabitation agreements are more common than they used to be, they still haven't resolved the financial uncertainties of a kept lover.

When the Man Is Being Kept

The focus here has been on the classic kept woman, but it's important to acknowledge that the opposite does occur. Women keep men for all the same reasons that men keep women: companionship, sex, security, and the economic wherewithal to be able to afford it.

There aren't as many women keeping men as the reverse, due to some very basic realities. Women have less money than men; fewer of them are able to support a lover. Plus, there are a lot more women than men at every point in the population age curve.

Nevertheless, male lovers exist. As with mistresses, they run the gamut from out-and-out golddiggers to paramours of decades-long devotion. Their perks and compensation are the same—cars, clothes, entertainment, travel.

The specifics of a relationship must be worked out by the individuals themselves. And women—especially divorced women living on alimony—must be attuned to the double-standard social implications of taking on a male lover. Courts have only recently begun to view these arrangements with less than a punitive eye.

It used to be that a man whose ex-wife had taken a permanent lover could go to court and argue for reduction or stoppage of alimony payments. Her behavior was often found to be "repugnant to sound morality." Today, rulings are more likely to reflect the tone of New Jersey's *Eames* v. *Eames:* "If support payments inure to the benefit of a paramour, it would be consistent with past court pronouncements to treat the matter no differently than if support payments were inuring to the benefit of any new party sharing the dwelling."

A Final, Non-Financial Consideration

Regardless of the financial benefits that may be enjoyed when one is the paramour of a wealthy man or woman, there is always a psychological price to pay. People who have been kept by others talk about the low self-esteem that invariably accompanies the situation. They are always second best to their lover's spouse, job, family. Their desire for stability and security can rarely be completely fulfilled. They must learn to be independent, yet they are permanently dependent upon another. They are an anomaly in an age of liberation, yet the inevitable adjunct to an era of affluence. For mistresses and male lovers—regardless of age, sex, or station in life—the piper will be paid.

 *Three*   # LIVING
TOGETHER

f you are cohabiting with someone, much of the information in the rest of this book will apply to you in a general way. However, there are special considerations for people who live together. Whether your relationship is relatively casual or has lasted longer than most marriages you can think of, don't assume that the monetary side of your situation doesn't need attention. Being careful with your finances can pay off in many ways. While you are together, it may help reinforce your romantic relationship. And if you end up going your separate ways after all, protecting your wallet will be your consolation prize.

BUDGETING AND BANKING

Figuring out how expenses will be shared and drawing up a budget require careful planning, periodic review and, if need be, revision. You should be confident that you are both living by the same fiscal rules.

Since most cohabiting couples have two incomes on which to draw, common arrangements include setting up a kitty for food and daily expenses and maintaining a joint checking account to pay for shared living expenses and purchases. In a typical case, each keeps a separate checking account and credit card for personal expenses—clothes, medical bills, presents, and the like. Cohabitants can't share health insurance policies or file joint tax returns; and a divorced parent may lose child support when he or she moves in with a new partner.

CREDIT

Credit is a fairly straightforward matter when you are single: You get it, use it, and pay for it.

Become one half of a couple, however (married or living together), and complications can crop up. The reason: Shared credit does not always equal shared debt. In fact, you risk jeopardizing your credit history and future borrowing power if you don't play your cards right when you team up.

What separates a married couple from an unmarried one?

Legal protection.

An extreme example: You give your live-in partner authorization to use your credit card. Then you break up. Your now ex-partner, however, continues to use your card—to the tune of $2,500 in merchandise. You cancel his/her privileges, but he/she refuses to reimburse you for those past charges.

What can you do? Legally, not a thing. You, and only you, are liable for the debt. (If you were married, you could at the very least make the debt figure part of the divorce negotiations.)

In fact, the only joint credit arrangement in which an unmarried has legal protection is when both partners sign a loan. Then you can sue the nonpaying partner for his/her share, often an expensive, protracted, and unpleasant affair.

The caveat in all this: Separate credit lines are best. (And "separate" is not a sign of mistrust—it's a sign of respect and regard for each partner's financial health.)

BUYING PROPERTY

Many couples eventually buy property together. Surprisingly, perhaps, single people buying a home together have proven to be among the safest mortgage risks. That serious a financial commitment presupposes an equally serious emotional one; nevertheless, smart couples make plans for disposing of the property in case they separate. Your real estate lawyer can draw up an agreement that protects each partner's interest.

COHABITATION AGREEMENTS

While anticipating a breakup may not add to your romance, protecting what belongs to you is important. If you combine households, itemize who bought the microwave, who donated the television, and the like. To avoid messy arguments later, decide on ownership when purchases are made and make a mutually prepared list.

The growth in the numbers of couples living together outside marriage—nearly 2 million, according to the U.S. Census Bureau—has led to the popularity of cohabitation agreements. These are the contractual cousins to prenuptial agreements—with several important differences.

The first is that prenuptial agreements are for people getting married, and cohabitation contracts are for people who are living together without marrying.

But the biggest difference is that cohabitation contracts are not as widely accepted in the courts, many of which maintain that living together is still legally "opposed to public policy."

At the same time, a cohabitation contract can be a future safeguard against a Lee Marvin-type "palimony" lawsuit, even in states that have not yet formally recognized live-in relationships.

In many ways, cohabitation contracts are much simpler than prenuptial agreements. A lawyer is not even required in most cases.

Various books (Merle H. Horwitz's *The Essential Guide to Living Together,* Quill, $4.95, is a good example) include sample forms that you can copy. The Horwitz book has a contract you can rip out, fill in the blanks, and sign at the bottom.

Basically, cohabitation contracts all say the same thing: "What's mine stays mine and what's yours stays yours."

In some complicated situations where funds are commingled—such as in joint bank accounts, shared investments, or buying a house together—it is advisable to seek legal counsel.

ESTATE PLANNING

It may seem that cohabitants need not bother with wills and estate planning. Not true. In all fifty states, if a "spouse equivalent" dies, the survivor has no legal right to any property held in the deceased's name, even if it was acquired jointly. Some states permit an oral contract to suffice as proof of joint ownership. Find out what laws apply in your state. In any event, if you want to share your estate, make a will.

BENEFITS

As a cohabitant, you can't receive government benefits based on family relationships. That means no Social Security, survivors', death, disability, or old-age benefits. Private employee benefits generally don't extend to unmarried couples, but you *can* name your partner as the beneficiary of your life insurance policy.

It used to be that a widow and widower who got together were usually better off remaining unmarried insofar as their Social Security benefits were concerned.

However, a recent series of changes in the law has removed that deterrent. Now, if a widow and widower marry, they will continue to receive the same amount they presently draw. In particular, the widow will retain her widow's benefit *unless* she would receive a higher amount based on her new husband's earnings. The easiest way to find out which amount would be greater is to have an employee at a local Social Security office make the calculations.

TAXES

Spouses are never considered dependents when it comes to taxes, but your live-in may qualify.

For a person to qualify as a dependent, he or she must meet each of five stiff tests. They are: member of household or relationship test; citizenship test; joint return test; gross income test; and support test.

- You can take an exemption for an unrelated person who lives with you for the entire year and is a member of your household. However, the relationship between you can't violate local law. (In some jurisdictions, cohabitation is still illegal.)
- A dependent has to be a U.S. citizen, resident or national, or a resident of Canada or Mexico for at least part of the year.
- You are not allowed this exemption for a dependent if he or she files a joint return.
- As a rule, you can't take this exemption unless your dependent's gross income was less than $1,000. (Gross income includes all income in the form of money, property, and services that is not exempt from tax.)
- The final test to meet is perhaps the toughest of all. You must provide *more than half* your dependent's support for that taxable year. To determine whether you furnished that amount, compare the amount of support you did provide with what he

or she received from all sources, including savings, benefits, salary, public assistance, and so on.

As you can see, the tests provide quite an obstacle and one, according to an IRS spokesperson, that most people can't overcome.

Note: You can get free tax advice from the IRS, but before you call (in person at a local office, if it's at all feasible) with this particular question, pull together all your records so you'll have the information at hand.

 **Four**

BEFORE
YOU TIE THE
KNOT . . .

 etting married (or remarried) is not only a romantic decision—it's a financial one as well. Before you tie the knot, here are some pointers to consider.

MARRY NOW, OR WAIT UNTIL NEXT YEAR?

For tax purposes, filing status (single or married) is determined as of the end of the year. Get married in December, and be treated as married for the entire year. Wait until January, and you're considered unmarried and cannot file a joint return for the previous year. Proper use of this rule can save a bundle in taxes.

Here's why. Single people are taxed at much higher rates—as much as 25 percent more than married couples with the same income. But the rates for a single person are lower than those imposed on a married couple where the husband and wife each have about the same income as the single person (or any combination that results in combined income for the couple that is about twice that of the single person).

THE COST OF GETTING MARRIED

Lady Diana Spencer's wedding in 1981 to Charles, Prince of Wales, was the greatest example of a fairy tale wedding since Princess Aurora was awakened by her prince in *Sleeping Beauty*.

Weddings of that grandeur are still the preserve of royalty, but traditional and even lavish weddings on a reduced scale are increasingly the choice of this decade's brides and grooms.

Much to the delight of florists, caterers, and wedding consultants everywhere, the formal wedding that most of today's first-time newlyweds pick is unquestionably more complicated, and expensive, than the simpler ceremonies of a few years back.

The number of weddings has increased by 9 percent since 1978, and there will be more weddings in the United States in the 1980s than during any other decade in history. If the trend continues, almost 24 million marriages will be celebrated by decade's end.

If you expect to participate in one of these galas, be prepared for expenditures that will make the average new home seem reasonable in price.

You can't avoid it: Getting married costs money. How much money depends on the kind of ceremony and reception you and your intended want to enjoy, what time of year you wed, where you live, the number of guests, and so on.

A wedding with 200 guests—which is the typical size, according to *Modern Bride* magazine—costs about $4,000, not including the reception. That $4,000 includes clothes, music, photography, flowers, rings, and other odds and ends, but no food and drink. Moreover, *Modern Bride* points out, almost half of all receptions have more guests than the wedding ceremony.

Clearly, the least expensive way to get married is to elope or, if you want to be more public, hold the ceremony at City Hall or the county courthouse. The cost: the price of the license, wedding rings, and the fee for the judge or justice of the peace.

If that seems spare and lacking in festivity, you simply have to plan to spend more. In fact, given the lifespan of some marriages these days, it's entirely possible that someone will be paying the bills for the wedding long after the divorce.

Times may change, but the conventions of traditional weddings remain immutable, including the division of financial responsibilities.

- The groom's shopping list encompasses the bride's engagement and wedding rings, the marriage license, clergy fees, bride's flowers, boutonnieres for the men in the wedding party, corsages for the two mothers, gifts for men in the wedding party, a bridal gift, hotel accommodations for out-of-town ushers, and the honeymoon.
- The groom's family picks up the tab for the rehearsal dinner.
- The bride buys a wedding ring and a gift for the groom, gifts for her attendants, and personal stationery. She also pays for hotel rooms for other women in her bridal party.
- The bride's parents pay for the wedding itself: invitations, announcements and enclosure cards, wedding dress and veil, accessories, flowers, photographs, fees for the church or synagogue, organist, and soloists. And that's just the ceremony. Also: transportation to and from the ceremony and the reception hall; the reception, including food, drink, music, flowers, and decorations; and the daughter's trousseau.

It may sound like an invitation to spend money, but conventional wisdom advises that you not economize on items that compromise your values. Your family may want to provide guests with a lavish dinner and unlimited drinks. For other families, tradition dictates punch or champagne, and cake. Obviously this is much cheaper, but to you it may not feel like a proper wedding. Avoid, even in a budget-conscious mood, settling for something you really don't like or feel comfortable with.

Determining an overall wedding budget and staying within it are immense challenges for any couple. As such, say the wags, it's a true test of being married. These general recommendations can help trim the price tag, however:

Choosing the Day

Marry in the off season. Selecting an off-season date can help you get a break on rental fees and other expenses associated with the reception. Couples still prefer June weddings, according to figures from the National Center for Health Statistics, but August and December are gaining in popularity as good times to tie the knot. That leaves nine other months to choose from.

The Honeymoon

In the same vein, choose an off-season honeymoon location. Bermuda in June, the Caribbean islands in January, Paris in July—all are romantic choices, but they are also expensive ones, given that seasonal high rates prevail at those times.

The Guest List

You can always trim the guest list. Even if you truly have no choice about inviting Aunt Sal or Cousin Jeff, clamp down on the number of friends your friends can bring. Instead of telling single friends to bring a guest, make clear that the invitation is for them alone.

Similarly, discourage friends and relatives with young children from assuming their offspring will be welcome—unless you are close to the children.

And justify to yourselves every name on the guest list. Don't invite all your office associates; dissuade your parents and those of your intended from using the event to repay all business and social obligations.

Sharing Expenses

The bride's family might want to explore the option of sharing costs with the groom's family. Since this is potentially an explosive topic that can tarnish future relations among all in-laws, broach this with great delicacy. In many instances, you may find it is no option at all.

As for budgeting specific costs, regional variations make calculating average costs for each item immensely difficult. Particularly for first marriages, though, the tab escalates quickly. If you and yours decide that eloping is out of the question, here's a broad outline of what to expect:

Clothes

Full bridal regalia is, as a rule, a once-in-a-lifetime purchase. Typically, the average bride visits ten to fifteen stores before selecting her dress. That much shopping gives a good idea of prevailing prices.

Prices at the low end start at a few hundred dollars. The upper limit? Well, Priscilla of Boston, one of the best, and best-known wedding dress designers, has been known to create gowns that sell for $30,000.

Add to your bill another $50 to $500 for the headpiece and veil. Here again, however, luxury knows no limits—you can spend thousands if you insist on hand beading and other intricate work.

Meanwhile, brides who have done this sort of thing before are advised against choosing a traditional wedding dress. This added flexibility about what to wear gives you increased control over what to pay. A dressy cocktail dress, an elegantly tailored cream-colored suit—you can shop around for these kinds of clothes at more familiar retailers.

Many men, on planning their wedding wardrobes, discover they own no formal wear—black tie or morning dress, for instance. If you have to rent, visit a number of shops before you sign a contract to get an idea of fees and quality of merchandise.

Rings

A ring is about as central to a wedding as the bride and groom. Still, you don't need a diamond-studded circlet to have the ceremony recognized before God and country. A simple gold band can be found for $100 or so—depending in part on the current price of gold. You can, of course, spend considerably more for carved or sculpted gold bands. Still, since this is one of the very few items from the wedding with any practical afterlife, select bands that you love and enjoy wearing.

If you consider an engagement incomplete without a ring, you can economize by getting one with a stone other than a diamond (or ruby or emerald). Good gems are expensive, period. No matter what you decide to buy, make your purchase from a reputable jeweler. If you buy anything on time, be clear about the financing terms.

Invitations

Social arbiters insist that there is only one correct kind of wedding invitation: engraved, with double envelopes. Printing costs vary, but you'll spend at least $100 for a hundred invitations.

While you're at your printers, look into buying announcements and stationery for thank-you notes. (Said social arbiters frown on sending folded notes with THANK YOU emblazoned on the front.)

Clergy

There is no standard fee for performing a wedding. In any event, you may want the minister, priest, or rabbi who has known you all your life to officiate, so what difference does it make if a colleague would perform the ceremony for $25 less? Do, however, plan to invite this person (and spouse, if applicable) to the reception, and ask whether you will have to pay any travel costs.

Flowers

When was the last time you ordered flowers? Then you have some idea of the staggering cost of floral displays.

Flowers for a wedding can easily cost thousands of dollars, especially if you want canopies, screens, and other intricate designs. Shop around for florists and ask to see samples of their work so you can compare not only prices but quality. If you use a hotel's reception rooms and catering service, don't be bullied into using the florist the hotel recommends. (Some hotels, however, sell package deals only.) And don't be shamed by a badgering florist into buying more flowers than you want or can afford.

Photographs

Memorializing the day in pictures or on videotape (or both) will not be cheap. Well-meaning amateurs generally are no substitute for professionals, who know how to pose portraits and compose sprightly candids. Here again, comparison shopping will help reveal which photographers can match their skills with your budget. You may be able to pay by the hour; more likely, you will pay for a package, including sittings, wedding and reception, proofs, and completed album. Cost: up to $4,000.

The Reception

If you thought deciding on every item up to now was complicated, you may want to pause a while. Planning the reception alone may persuade you to elope.

Among the factors to weigh:

- Reception hall: Anywhere from fifty to hundreds of dollars, depending on size, location, and grandness. For the Knights of Columbus or VFW hall you can expect a low rent. At the other extreme, many hotels don't charge for the actual room if they do the catering. A restaurant may charge you for the space plus the food and service.

- Food and drink: Do you have a full dinner and open bar in mind? Expect to spend anywhere from $25 to $200 per person.
- Entertainment: When hiring musicians, be aware that you may have to pay union scale. With that in mind, hire the minimum necessary to provide the sound and volume you want.
- Incidentals: Matchbooks and napkins, centerpieces, wedding cake, towels for the rest rooms—the list is endless, or at least it seems that way. Still, these items can add up to big money, so keep track of what you spend.

Deductible Wedding Expenses

Wedding expenses generally are non-deductible personal expenses. But if you have a wedding reception, any sales tax paid to the restaurant or caterer is deductible.

In most cases, parents pick up the tab for the wedding. If their income is higher than that of the newlyweds, the deduction is worth more to them than to the young couple. But if the parents are retired or otherwise have less income than the young couple, it is preferable for tax purposes to have the children hire and pay the caterer themselves.

A young married couple is likely also to spend quite a bit on furniture and appliances. These are subject also to sales tax, which is deductible.

If the parents pick up the tab for these items but want the kids to get the tax deduction (again, advisable if the kids are in a higher tax bracket), they can make a cash gift to the children, permitting them to pay for the items directly.

Any donation you make to the church is also deductible. But it's important to note the difference between a voluntary donation and a fee or other required payment. For example, a fee charged by the minister or a charge for the use of the chapel doesn't qualify as a deduction.

PRENUPTIAL AGREEMENTS

Sam, a forty-five-year-old businessman, and Janet, a twenty-nine-year-old advertising executive, decided to get married last year. It was the second marriage for Sam, a millionaire who earns more than $200,000 a year, and the first for Janet, who earns about $30,000.

"But first, sweetheart," Sam cooed into her ear one night a few weeks before the wedding, "let's make a prenuptial agreement. It's just a simple contract my lawyer can write up for us. It will make sure you and the kids from my first marriage are taken care of if we ever break up or something happens to me."

Janet thought about it. She had misgivings about a contract anticipating the failure of a marriage that hadn't even begun, and she resented the implication that she was after Sam's money. But she agreed with Sam's logic, and he had been burned when he and his first wife were divorced.

Janet and Sam went to his lawyer and had a prenuptial agreement drawn up. It provided that in the event of divorce or Sam's death, Janet would get 30 percent of the property and investments they acquired during their marriage. The rest—including Sam's stocks, bonds, his house in the country, and the jewelry from his mother—would go to his children.

When Janet and Sam signed the agreement, two days before they were married, they joined the tens of thousands of American couples each year who are signing prenuptial agreements—also called antenuptial agreements or simply marriage contracts.

The specter of divorce is leading increasing numbers of brides and grooms—especially those who have been through it before—to turn to prenuptial agreements as a legal means of protecting themselves both financially and emotionally.

In fact, the rise in prenuptial agreements parallels the rise in the nation's divorce rate: about 1 million marriages will break up this year.

The prenuptial agreement is really just a legal contract that outlines the division of property in the event of divorce or death. In death or divorce, it can, in effect, waive each spouse's claims on the other's property, superseding a will or state laws.

Prenuptial agreements are most popular in second or third marriages, among couples where one prospective spouse has considerably more assets or income than the other. In a typical case, the spouse with more assets has children from a previous marriage to share in the estate.

A simple prenuptial agreement may cost as little as $200, but a tycoon recently paid a Park Avenue lawyer $35,000 for a book-length agreement establishing various complicated trusts involving hundreds of investments and corporate holdings.

Men more often than women are the ones seeking prenuptial agreements. But as more women move into executive positions and their earnings rise—and social taboos against older women marrying younger men crumble—the number of brides insisting on prenuptial agreements is increasing.

Some couples scrimp by hiring just one lawyer, but in anything more than the simplest agreement, the husband and wife should each have one. Cecile Weich, a prominent New York attorney, says, "Lovers make the best bargains, but lawyers make the best bargainers."

Both men and women, however, are reluctant to discuss publicly their prenuptial agreements. That's why Sam's and Janet's full names are not used here and why a young woman in Texas says, "I'm embarrassed for anyone else to know that we needed one. It's very personal."

That woman, intent on protecting her inheritance, had a prenuptial agreement drawn up without telling her husband first. He was hurt and angry initially, but now both say that fully discussing their finances helped them avoid the money arguments that plague many young couples.

Traditionally, the prenuptial agreement was the province of the rich only. But no more. Lawyers across the country say more and more people from the middle class are writing them too. Some attorneys predict that within a few years one of every three couples getting married will have a prenuptial agreement.

But that is not to say that everyone needs one. First-time brides and grooms in their early twenties, for example, with few assets and relatively equal incomes, have no need for a prenuptial agreement. It is possible, however, that they might need one later. If one or both spouses, for instance, come into a lot of money or property, they may want to consider a postnuptial agreement years after they've exchanged their vows. It's the same thing as a prenuptial agreement and just as binding in court.

The law historically has frowned on prenuptial agreements. Any contract that contemplated divorce was "opposed to public policy." Today, no state flatly bars prenuptial agreements, though the courts in every state retain the right to review them. (Technically, a prenuptial agreement doesn't really become enforceable until death or divorce.) Judges will generally throw out an agreement only in cases of duress, fraud, or misrepresentation.

An example of duress, the courts have held, is when a man slips his bride-to-be a prenuptial agreement at the rehearsal dinner and whispers, "Sign it, honey, or the wedding is off."

Fraud is considerably harder to prove. In one case a judge upheld a prenuptial agreement, saying it didn't matter that the husband mentioned it only *after* the wedding invitations were in the mail and the wife hadn't had the benefit of separate legal counsel.

Most successful challenges to prenuptial agreements, however, are for misrepresentation: One spouse doesn't disclose all his or her assets and income.

There are also examples of courts tossing out prenuptial agreements that did not anticipate changed circumstances. An Ohio court recently voided a 1969 prenuptial agreement that had limited the wife to $200 per month for ten years—the newlyweds had never dreamed he would become a Pepsi-Cola distributing executive with a six-figure income.

Finally, courts also occasionally overturn prenuptial agreements simply because they are unfair. In a recent case in Indiana, the court voided a prenuptial agreement that gave the wife a one-time payment of $5,000. The judge said she was entitled to a larger share of her husband's $3 million and awarded her $188,500.

Courts are loath to enforce nonfinancial clauses of prenuptial agreements—even though there is no limit on what can be included. (One offbeat clause specified that *she* use the left half and *he* the right half of the medicine cabinet.) But people who write prenuptial agreements can count on just about any fair and reasonable financial provision being upheld. One agreement required that the husband continue to pay his wife's dog's veterinary bills. Another provided for alternate-performance custody of the couple's season tickets to the ballet. And an American woman who married an Arab sheik had an agreement that required her husband to pay transportation and medical costs so each of their children would be born in a hospital in the United States. That agreement also required the sheik to establish a $500,000 trust fund for each child.

William Zabel, an attorney who has written hundreds of prenuptial agreements in New York and Florida, says, "An agreement can be the constitution of the marriage. It can also save legal fees and emotional strain later by setting up the rules for a divorce, including who moves out during the separation. There's not so much to fight about since both sides know what to do."

Zabel says, for example, that a prenuptial agreement might have headed off the bitter court battle and sordid publicity surrounding the recent seamy Pulitzer divorce trial in Florida. He and many lawyers say prenuptial agreements actually help some divorcing spouses part on friendly terms.

Some agreements provide that one spouse—inevitably, the poorer one—gets a lump-sum payment upon divorce or the death of the other. Others specify a percentage. In some cases the percentages gradually change, moving toward 50–50 the longer the marriage lasts. One young doctor and his wife made a prenuptial agreement that upon divorce provided her $2,000 for each year of the marriage. If the marriage had lasted 15 years, though, the prenuptial agreement expired. (It turned out to be a five-year, $10,000 marriage.)

Some lawyers also recommend that prenuptial agreements include clauses prohibiting one spouse from claiming part of the other's future earnings when they divorce.

When there is no prenuptial agreement, state law applies. In most states, that means the surviving spouse must get at least one-third or one-half of the other's estate upon death. And it means that in divorce cases, most state courts will either divide the property acquired during marriage down the middle or try to split it according to each partner's contribution. Incidentally, more and more courts are viewing home duties such as cleaning and child care as financial contributions.

But the negotiations necessary for most prenuptial agreements beg tough questions:

Is it emotionally healthy for a couple to be planning for divorce even before they get married? Does talking about divorce make it more likely to happen someday? Or is it a healthy way of outlining a life together? Shouldn't any marriage be strong enough to survive a little practical thinking?

"A prenuptial agreement is very important for most people getting married the second time, when they're older and better able to handle it," Dr. Joyce Brothers the psychologist says. "But a prenuptial agreement for people getting married the first time can be a disaster. When you start talking about divorce, it's not just a vague idea anymore. It's a possibility. You go into marriage knowing you might divorce instead of thinking it's going to last forever."

While few unhappy spouses would ever admit it, some may stick with marriages largely because their prenuptial agreements would lower their standard of living if they divorced, according to some lawyers.

And a West Virginia woman says she found an unexpected benefit from a prenuptial agreement—she and her husband's children by his previous marriage got along better once they knew she was not cutting them out of his will.

Some lawyers advise clients not to write prenuptial agreements if it might get the marriage off on the wrong foot. It's a common story: A couple comes in for a prenuptial agreement, starts arguing, and ends up calling off the ceremony.

"But in a way, that can be good," Cindra Carson, an Eau Claire, Wisconsin, attorney says. "Maybe they shouldn't get married in the first place."

Is a Prenuptial Agreement for You?

If you're getting married, it's worth considering whether a prenuptial agreement is appropriate for you and your spouse-to-be.

If you answer yes to any of these questions, you may be a good candidate. Consult your attorney for more details.

1) Do you have children from a previous marriage?
2) Are you in line to receive a large inheritance that for some reason you do not wish to share with your new spouse?
3) Is there a wide divergence in earnings and/or assets between you and your future spouse, or do you expect there to be one in the future?
4) Can you keep your emotions and finances separate; do you wish to?

But keep in mind, prenuptial agreements can be fraught with emotional pitfalls. If you find your anxiety/hostility level rising instead of receding, at the mere thought of such an agreement, better drop the idea completely.

Five   # MARRIAGE

o you think love and marriage go together, and you've made your trip to the altar. Congratulations! But getting married is, of course, only the beginning. *Staying married* is today's challenge.

Despite today's divorce rate, getting married is not something most people enter into lightly. Becoming romantically involved is one thing, but becoming a married couple—a social, legal, financial unit—is something else altogether.

Now that you are married, your financial needs and burdens will change. To give you and yours the best shot at wedded bliss, you will need to deal realistically and competently with your mutual money matters. Making money, spending it, and managing it are so important in any serious relationship that we've given these subjects separate chapters of their own. This chapter will cover other financial matters particular to marriage that can make the difference between marrying for richer—or poorer.

PLAN AHEAD

To get your marriage off to a sound start, establish good communication and cooperative planning in all areas—especially financial.

Discuss your goals and priorities for tomorrow, next year, and the years ahead. These can range from buying your own home to raising children to starting your own business. Whatever your goals are, identify them and aim to work together to attain them.

Investments: before you actually make any, be sure to:

- Set aside funds for emergencies and make sure health, life, house, and car insurance needs are covered.
- Determine your temperament for risk. Does the idea of risking money for a potentially higher return make you lose sleep?
- Carve at least these rules of investing into your memory: 1) become knowledgeable; 2) realize the risks of what you're getting into; 3) don't take advice or tips without investigating them yourself; 4) diversify.

YOU GET MARRIED

Your friends and relatives aren't the only people who should be sent wedding announcements. You should also notify anyone involved with your finances that your status is changing.

Rearrange Your Financial Affairs

First, take care of the routine business:

- Talk to your insurance agents and employment benefits specialists to make sure you are not paying for overlapping life, health, and other insurance coverage (more about this in Chapter 6);
- Notify the Social Security Administration of your marriage so

you'll be eligible for your spouse's benefits (more about this in a moment);

- Write or rewrite your will as necessary to include your new spouse;
- Add your spouse as beneficiary on your company pension and profit-sharing plans;
- A woman who changes her name at marriage should make the change on her driver's license, credit cards, employment records, and all other identification.

Establishing joint checking and savings (or money market) accounts can give you more borrowing and investment power. This is particularly important for a wife who will be a homemaker. If you both work, you should decide how much each of you will deposit in both accounts every payday. The amount put into your checking account should be enough to cover fixed monthly expenses, and allow for an accumulation of savings. (For more about banking, see Chapter 8.)

This is only the beginning.

MARRIAGE AND TAXES

We all know that taxes are a fact of life. Unpleasant though the task may be, it's worth the effort to take the time to understand exactly how being married affects your tax situation. By familiarizing yourself with current tax laws regarding marriage, you could save yourself a bundle. Watch tax law changes!

Is It Better to File Jointly or Separately?

In most cases, a married couple filing a joint return will pay less tax than if each spouse files separately.

If both of you work, you can take the two-earner married couple deduction, but you have to file jointly to do so. This deduction is 10 percent of the earned income of the spouse with the lower earnings, up to a maximum deduction of $3,000 (more about this below).

One situation where filing separate returns may be advantageous is if the family income all comes from investments and is divided equally between husband and wife. If one of the spouses had substantial medical expenses, the 5 percent floor (above which medical expenses are deductible) might bar a medical deduction on a joint return but yield a deduction on the separate return.

Special Tax Break for Working Couples

Back in 1981, Congress provided some relief from the "marriage penalty tax," at least when the husband and wife both work.

If a husband and wife both earn income, on their joint return they can deduct 10 percent of the earned income of the lower-earning spouse up to $30,000: maximum deduction, $3,000. Any deductible contributions by the lower-earning spouse to an IRA or Keogh plan reduce by that amount the spouse's earnings for figuring the 10 percent deduction.

Example: The lower-earning spouse earns $8,000 of self-employment income and contributes $2,000 of it to an IRA and $1,200 to a Keogh plan. That reduces the $8,000 of earnings to $4,800 for computing the special 10 percent deduction, which would be $480. This gives the couple a total of $3,680 of deductions on their joint return (the $3,200 plus $480), just from three sources alone.

Income Averaging

Many non-working spouses are reentering the job market. The addition of a second income to the joint return may sharply expand taxable income. Check whether it qualifies you to compute your tax using the *income averaging method*, which in effect enables you to spread the current year's increased income over a four-year period. It could lower your tax.

First step: You determine your average annual taxable income for the three prior years. Second step: Increase this average sum by 40 percent. You qualify for income averaging if your taxable income for the current year exceeds by more than $3,000 the sum you calculated in step two. Every year you qualify you can use income averaging.

Hiring Your Spouse

If you run a business as a corporation or as a self-employed individual, hiring your spouse to help can be an easy way to convert an additional $1,750 of annual income into deferred income. If a wife, for instance, helps her husband in his firm, putting her on the payroll for $2,000 will permit the tax saving.

As an employee she is entitled to contribute $2,000 to her own Individual Retirement Account. (If she had had no earnings, the husband could only contribute $2,250 to a spousal IRA for both, thus the $1,750 savings.)

Warning: The $2,000 earnings that the employee spouse includes in his or her income will not get the benefit of the special 10 percent deduction allowed for two-earner married couples. In computing the amount subject to the 10 percent deduction, the lower-earning spouse must reduce earnings by the $2,000 contributed to his or her IRA.

Taxes and Long-distance Marriage

To be entitled to deduct travel expenses you must be "away from home." But the IRS says that for tax purposes your "home" is not necessarily where your immediate family lives or what you otherwise think of as home. For travel deduction purposes, your home is your place of business, employment, or post of duty. In today's mobile society, this rule sometimes creates unusual results.

Larry and Betty Thomas maintain their home in St. Louis. Betty is a vice-president of a local department store. Larry is an executive with an airline. Last year, the airline moved Larry to a new position in Dallas. He has arranged his schedule to fit into a four-day work week in Dallas. On Sunday evenings he hops a flight from St. Louis to Dallas, returning home on Thursday night. He has a studio apartment in Dallas.

While Larry thinks of St. Louis as his home, Dallas is his home for travel purposes. This means that the cost of his apartment and other expenses in Dallas cannot be deducted. Larry is only "away from home" from Friday to Sunday. But because this travel is personal (i.e., to be with his family), Larry again gets no deduction.

The twist is that if the airline has Larry attend a one-day meeting in St. Louis, then he is away from home and entitled to deduct expenses—his pro-rata portion of one day's household expenses, etc.

Taking Your Spouse on a Business Trip

Chances are your spouse can present any number of valid reasons why he or she should go along on a business trip to a resort area. No need to fret about the cost. You should be able to take your husband or wife along on the trip without refinancing the mortgage on your house.

To begin with, taking your spouse along doesn't double the cost. Many hotels charge the same room rate for single or double occupancy. Others add only a nominal surcharge for a second person in the room. If you are there on business, you can deduct the full single-occupant rate, not just one-half of the rate for a double. Similarly, if you are driving, the full cost (gas, tolls, etc.) is deductible even though your spouse is along just for the ride.

Moreover, if you have a valid business purpose for your spouse's attendance on the trip, you may be able to deduct all of his or her expenses. But be prepared for close scrutiny by the IRS. If you are audited, the examiner will want to know whether your spouse's presence was *necessary*. The fact that his/her presence was *helpful*, for example to handle secretarial chores, will not suffice, nor will the excuse that you needed an escort to an association dinner.

The courts may be more lenient, though. Roy Disney, for example, head of Disney Studios, traveled with his wife. The federal court of appeals of the ninth circuit ruled that because of the company's image of family entertainment, it was appropriate for Mrs. Disney to be with her husband when he met with business contacts.

MARRIAGE AND SOCIAL SECURITY

You don't have to be old to love Social Security. In addition to its being a retirement fund, it is also life insurance, disability insurance, and an indirect way to help care for your elderly relatives.

Is it the whole answer to your retirement or insurance program? Of course not. Nor was it ever meant to be. But it is still a bargain and, for most Americans, a better package of family protection than you could buy on your own.

Social Security as Life Insurance

It was when Mike died at age forty that Dan became aware of Social Security in more than just a casual way. As an accountant, a next-door neighbor, and a good friend, Dan went with Mike's widow, Kim, when she went to the Social Security office to apply for survivors' benefits for herself and the two children.

What he noted made a distinct impression on him because the statistics of his life paralleled those of Mike's.

Both had about the same level of earnings throughout their adult lives—about the maximum amount covered by Social Security in just about every year. Up until the time of his death, Mike had paid a total of $17,396 in Social Security taxes (which had been matched by employers over the years.)

What could Kim and the children, aged fourteen and eleven expect to get, Dan wondered.

The benefits were laid out. Starting with the month of Mike's death, Kim and the children became eligible for benefits of $1,260 a month, an amount that will be kept up-to-date with increases in the cost of living. The children's benefits will continue while they are in school—up to their eighteenth birthdays.

The portion of the family Social Security check payable to

Kim for having the children in her care will stop when the younger child reaches sixteen. In the meantime, if she should go to work and earn more than the "exempt amount"—an estimated $5,400 in 1985 and $5,760 in 1986 (the "exempt amount" is tied to the cost of living)—the total benefit would also be affected. But each child will still receive $539 a month up to age eighteen.

Even if she works, Kim will again become eligible for benefits at age sixty—though benefits could start as early as age fifty if she were to become disabled.

Altogether, by the time the children are grown, Mike's family stands to collect a total of $86,400 in Social Security benefits— about five times more than the $17,396 he paid out of his earnings before his death.

Social Security is not *just* a retirement income; *it's life insurance protection worth thousands of dollars to young families.*

Social Security as Disability Protection

Social Security pays benefits to a worker who is permanently disabled for work or has a disability so severe that it is expected to keep him or her from any substantial gainful activity for at least a year. Disability benefits are payable to the worker, to his or her young children, and to the worker's spouse at age sixty-two, or regardless of age if she or he is caring for the children.

If you, as a young man or woman, think you will be paying Social Security taxes for many, many years before you will collect anything, we hope you are right. But consider this—42 percent of today's young men will either die or become disabled and lose substantial time from work before age sixty-five. For young women, the risk of death or disability before sixty-five is 28 percent.

Social Security and Retirement

Dan, the good neighbor, expects to make it to retirement age. Given an average life expectancy, he and his wife (who at this point has never worked outside the home) can look forward to receiving retirement benefits that will be worth $658,076 when he attains age sixty-five. Between now and his retirement at age sixty-five, he will have paid $308,002 in Social Security taxes toward his Old Age and Survivors' Insurance (OASI) protection.

Born in 1959

John works as a troubleshooter on the computer terminals used to issue tickets for the ice shows, concerts, hockey games, and other sports events held in the city's new civic center. He earns $15,000 a year—about average for all workers covered under Social Security. This includes the money he makes during the weekend playing guitar in a rock band.

The weekend gigs are about to end, though, because Natalie, the lead singer, has just finished her studies in advanced Russian and is about to take a translator's job overseas.

Assuming they both continue in their present tracks with John an average earner and Natalie with earnings around or above the Social Security maximum earning base, John will get a 172 percent return on the OASI portion of the Social Security taxes he will pay between now and his retirement in the year 2025. Natalie will get a 148 percent return.

The Social Security benefit formula is weighted in favor of the lower-income worker.

Born in 1919

Soon Joe and Vivian will be somewhere in New Mexico, riding around the mesas in their new recreational vehicle (RV). Joe retired in 1985 from his position as head of the circulation department of a newspaper.

Joe, who was earning over the $37,800 Social Security maximum earnings base when he retired, shakes his head when he recalls that when he started working in the late 1930s, the maximum was only $3,000 a year—and only about 4 percent of the people covered by Social Security then were making more than

$3,000 a year. He has been lucky, he thinks. He has always earned wages at or above the maximum covered by Social Security.

Joe is collecting a Social Security benefit of $775 a month. Vivian, who is the same age and who has worked sporadically in part-time and short-term jobs, will get $387—an amount equal to half of Joe's benefit.

In total, Joe paid $38,137 in Social Security taxes (OASI only)—and that includes the interest his contributions would have earned if invested. His and Vivian's benefits will amount to $215,680 over the fifteen years following his retirement—the average life expectancy of a sixty-five-year-old man. Vivian can be expected to outlive him by about five years.

Younger workers will not get as big a return as Joe and Vivian, and there will be single people who will die just short of retirement age, leaving no survivors eligible for benefits from Social Security taxes they paid.

But the vast majority of today's entrants into the work force can look forward to receiving their money's worth in retirement and disability protection for themselves and in survivors' protection for their families.

Beyond that, if it were not for the payments the program is making now to their parents, grandparents, and elderly uncles and aunts, money would no doubt be coming out of the pockets of people now working—directly, or in additional taxes to support the welfare rolls.

Social Security is a covenant between generations. It is and always must be a promise that will be kept. And it's a program that will give you your money's worth.

Social Security and Remarriage

Q: I simply don't understand the rules for Social Security pertaining to first wives and second wives. I have been married to my husband for sixteen years. Previously he was married to another woman for sixteen years and then divorced. She has worked sporadically. I have always worked, though I never earned as much as my husband does. All children are grown. If he dies, who gets his Social Security—she or I? Or does my share get cut in half? None of the printed material ever seems to explain this.

A: Both you and the former wife would be eligible, upon your husband's death, to collect benefits based on his record of earnings. These Social Security benefits are payable beginning at age sixty (or as early as age fifty if the woman is totally disabled) to a widow and also to a divorced widow—if the dissolved marriage lasted at least ten years.

The payment of benefits to your husband's divorced wife would have no effect at all on your benefits. The so-called "family maximum provision," which limits the amount that can be paid out on a worker's Social Security earnings record, does not apply where a divorced spouse's benefits are involved.

As your husband's present, legal wife, living with him at the time of his death, you would collect the $255 lump-sum death benefit as well.

Note that as a wife who has worked and built up her own record of earnings, the benefits payable to you at age sixty-two or later will consist of your own retired worker's benefit plus any difference between the amount of that benefit and the wife's or widow's benefit based on your husband's Social Security record, if higher. In effect, you will get the higher of the two benefits, but not both. This would be the case whether or not there was a divorced widow in the picture.

Q: There is a chance that my husband's first wife may remarry. Could she still collect divorced widow's benefits based on his Social Security record if that should happen?

A: Yes, if the remarriage does not take place until she has reached age sixty (or age fifty in the case of a disabled widow). Under a change in the law that became effective this past January, a surviving divorced widow who remarries at sixty or later can continue to receive benefits based on the earnings of a divorced husband.

Should she remarry before she reaches sixty, however, she would lose her right to benefits as a divorced spouse—unless the new marriage terminated. In that case, she could once again become eligible for benefits based on her earlier husband's record of earnings.

It may sound complicated, but the purpose is clear—to provide a safety net for one of the poorest segments of our population. The poverty rate for older women is about 65 percent higher than for older men. One-third of all widows live below the poverty line and they live there a long, long time—an average of eighteen years. Displaced homemakers divorced after long-standing marriages are particularly vulnerable.

(For more on Social Security and divorce, see Chapter 9.)

Are Your Social Security Records Correct?

The Social Security recordkeeping system is not infallible. Your earnings could end up in someone else's account or fail to be recorded at all, which would mean less insurance for you now and lower retirement benefits later.

Don't let this happen to you!

It's easy enough to check. Pick up a pre-addressed "Request for Social Security Statement of Earnings" form at your local Social Security office, or call and ask the office to send you one. Complete and mail the form. Within four to six weeks you should receive a statement of the earnings credited to your Social Security account.

Check these figures against copies of your past W-2 forms. Only those earnings subject to Social Security tax will appear on the statement. If you think an error has been made, contact your local Social Security office. The office will investigate it and help you receive proper credit.

Warning: Errors that occurred over three years, three months, and fifteen days ago may not be amendable, since the federal statute of limitations expires at that time.

It's wise to check every two or three years.

MARRIAGE AND CHILDREN

Deciding to Have a Child

Behind that cuddly, lovable, cherished infant is an awesome responsibility and a staggering financial commitment.

Whether it's directly—through food, pediatricians, cub or brownie scout uniforms, piano lessons, sneakers, schools, toys, and the like—or indirectly—through larger housing, more hot water for baths, larger phone bills, increased insurance coverage, child care, and more—you will be paying dearly.

Those costs are only part of the economic story. If a working mother has to leave work to rear a child, that means lost family income—not to mention the possibility of lost skills if the woman is working in a rapidly changing career area. In many cases, mothers who had planned to take off a year or more to rear a child or children have returned to work after a matter of months because both husband and wife feel too pressured by the loss of the two salaries to which they have become accustomed. Nearly 70 percent of new mothers who take leave from work are back on the job within four months after giving birth. If the wife does go back to work and you pay someone other than a family member to care for your child, you probably are entitled to a tax credit.

That's why wives and husbands have to decide whether they should postpone having kids until they're economically better prepared—or have fewer children. Or should the wife postpone her career until their last child is at least in kindergarten?

Before you sway under the weighty figures of child rearing, know that the costs start off manageable. Even though the experience of giving birth—hospital, routine delivery—may run around $2,500, most health/major medical insurance policies cover a large portion of this. But make certain you have the maternity benefits *before* the pregnancy. Once the wife is pregnant, it is too late to get or to increase maternity benefits on your health insurance.

And while the cost of baby clothes, special formulas, equipment, and nurses may seem burdensome now, know that expenses really climb in the teen years—reaching about 200 percent higher around the age of seventeen or eighteen than in the birth year.

How can you plan for this rise? It's hard. You can put gift money that you don't need now into a special savings account (or, if substantial enough, into a money market account) with you as the custodian, to be used as you need it for the child's support, or saved toward a specific goal such as college. The taxes on the interest are usually nonexistent because they are based on the child's tax bracket.

There are now mutual funds specifically designed to help you provide financial security for a child through long-term investment.

As soon as your baby is born, add him or her to your health/major medical insurance, reassess your life insurance and disability insurance needs, revamp your budget (the "entertainment" category now includes a good babysitter), and revise your will.

The Blended Family

Conflicts of financial interest most commonly occur in a second marriage when former spouses and children are involved.

He may want a new car, but her child needs braces.

She may want a Caribbean vacation, but he needs the money to make an alimony payment.

The variations are endless and can be explosive threats unless financial obligations are understood and accepted from the outset.

Two emotional pitfalls that can lead to financial tension in a second marriage:

- Resentment of alimony payments: Unless you and your spouse want to enter a court and battle for renegotiation—for which you'll pay dearly both emotionally and financially—you simply must accept alimony as a fixed monthly expense. Make paying it as routine, unemotional, and automatic as paying the rent or telephone bill.
- Resentment of child-care costs: Children, from the cradle to college, are expensive. Whether they are yours or not, providing for them is part of the responsibility and reality of a second marriage.

If you do have children from a previous marriage, you may want to make special provisions for them in your will. One option is to set up a trust that enables a remarried person to bequeath income interest in property to a spouse without giving him or her actual control over the property. Instead, these trusts designate that the principal passes on to the children after the death of the heir. In this way you make certain that after your death, your second spouse is financially taken care of, but that ultimately your estate will pass to your children from your first marriage.

Dealing with your spouse's or your own "past life" in a new marriage can be difficult at times. The less you dwell on and resist the expenses stemming from a previous marriage, the better off you'll be.

If you find it hard to put the past in its place, consider turning to a self-help group, family counselor, a trusted friend, or a local chapter of The Stepfamily Association of America. This national not-for-profit organization provides educational and emotional support to stepfamilies. For information, send a self-addressed stamped envelope to: Stepfamily Association of America, 28 Allegheny Ave., Baltimore, MD 21204.

Six # MAKING MONEY

nless you're independently wealthy, earning a living probably takes up most of your days—and perhaps nights as well. And you worry. You worry about making enough money, about where your career is going, about losing your job, about changing jobs, about that guy at work who is nothing but trouble, about that unfair remark your boss made, about firing your assistant, about that important meeting tomorrow. . . . Multiply these tensions by two for a two-earner couple, and you have a lot of stress put on a relationship.

It's not all bad news, however. Hopefully, you enjoy what you do and get a charge out of doing it well. A two-paycheck arrangement has obvious financial benefits and psychological bonuses as well.

Herewith some tips on avoiding the pitfalls of a two-earner romance and on making the most of its advantages.

WHEN SHE EARNS MORE THAN HE

When she earns more than he is it role reversal? Or role confusion?

Often, some of both.

In such a relationship, not only are traditional sex roles turned upside down, but each partner's self-image may be shaken as well.

Her *head* says her role as chief breadwinner is something to be proud of, but she may *feel* exploited when she turns over $100 for her mate's new shoes.

His head may tell him that being a sculptor is more important than earning a six-figure income, but his self-worth may wither as he loses financial dominance.

As women's salaries edge upward, the dilemma of how to handle the emotional issues in a relationship in which the woman assumes the dominant earning role is a real and present concern for many people.

We interviewed couples to discover exactly what the problems are when she earns more than he, how they can best be resolved, and why these solutions work.

Take Dianne and Bill. (All names have been changed.) When they first moved in together eight years ago, they were deeply committed to the separate-but-equal financial doctrine. (This is not unusual for single men and women who have been financially independent for a number of years.) Each maintained a separate bank account. Each maintained and paid for a separate car, telephone, collection of books, records and, as it turned out, vacuum cleaner. Financial togetherness consisted of a drawer into which bills and receipts were thrown for common expenses such as rent, food, and entertainment. At the end of the month, one person wrote out the checks for mutual expenses and asked the other for half the amount. This arrangement reflected both an uncertainty about the future and a fear of being committed for the wrong reasons. As Dianne put it, "I didn't want us to stay together because we owned a stove together."

At the time, Dianne and Bill were both college professors earning about the same amount. There were few conflicts. Then their circumstances changed: They married. Dianne put herself through law school and landed a job at a prestigious, high-pressure law firm. They bought a condominium. While Bill continued to teach about twenty hours a week, Dianne was putting in fifteen-hour days and earning $15,000 more than her husband. For Dianne, a series of tensions developed around money. Bill, interviewed separately, maintained that he and Dianne have never had any substantial disagreements over money. "I spend more easily," he said, "and I think I've loosened her up a bit when it comes to parting with a dollar."

Dianne remembers matters differently. "When I was earning a lot more, I felt I wanted to have more say about where the money went. I became resentful about a whole series of things. First, I was putting in these incredibly hard days. I began to feel, 'I'm slaving and he's not,' and had no tolerance for things not going my way. On top of that, Bill was getting used to the standard of living I was creating. He kept buying expensive things for himself. So I began to feel, 'While I'm working late every night earning our bread, he's out spending it.' On the other hand, I didn't want to be the one who always said 'No.' That didn't feel right either."

What was going on?

To begin with, according to Dr. George Landberg, a New York psychiatrist who specializes in working with couples, Dianne felt intuitively that what was being set up was a child-parent relationship, but she did not want to play the role of mommy. One solution, Dr. Landberg suggests, would be to state clearly what their common account was for and to restate the fact that each person's separate account was for each person's private needs.

However, another conflict was also taking place. Phyllis Schiff, a Rochester, New York, family therapist, believes that women who earn more than their male partners are often in the midst of a psychological no-win situation. "Underneath the rhetoric of women's liberation, women reared in the old social patterns have not changed enough yet. They still connect earning power with masculinity. Many women who make more money than their husbands or lovers have an underlying concern that they are being used."

How, in fact, did Dianne and Bill resolve their conflicts? Dianne believes they never totally resolved them. Instead, she changed the situation by *choosing a less demanding job and earning less money*.

If Schiff is correct when she observes that "women must come to terms with their traditional values and, when it comes to earning power, their own inability to accept equal roles," then Dianne's decision, conscious or unconscious, makes sense. It may not be ideal or, in some cases, possible, but it underscores the expressed wish of every couple interviewed—for an *equality* of income. Clearly, this is perceived as their ideal.

The woman's concern about "being used" was even more dramatically illustrated in the relationship of Anne and Tom. They met and married while both were working for a government agency and earning equal salaries. Anne was thirty-two and a lawyer. Tom was forty-three and an architect. It was a second marriage for each.

Tom's first marriage had been based on the "unspoken assumption that everything went into the same pot and you had to clear expenditures with the other partner." After their divorces, Anne and Tom each enjoyed paying their own bills and accounting to no one. When they married, they maintained separate checking accounts and a mutual money fund account. Anne paid the joint bills and charged Tom half. For three years they split everything 50–50, including buying a piece of land. According to Anne, "Everything went beautifully." Then the entire financial picture changed. They had a child, and their expenses rose. Anne went into private practice; her income soared. Tom decided to go into business for himself. They both agreed that for a year Tom did not have to contribute money to the household. Anne began paying all the bills from her earnings. Even when Tom's business began to turn a profit, Anne continued to support the household. An unspoken assumption had developed: What was left over after Tom's alimony and child support expenses was his spending money. Occasionally, Tom would throw a chunk of cash into their savings account, but not on a regular basis.

Anne now says that when Tom went into business, they both had expected that one day he would "make it big" and she would "just earn a good salary." The opposite has taken place. Anne has become a resounding success, able to buy herself a mink coat and nearly anything else she desires, while Tom's business has not fared well. Nor does Tom participate in household chores as Anne believes a woman would. Today, Anne not only feels exploited—she's beginning to wonder if her husband hasn't worked hard enough to make his business a success *because* she's such a financial winner. In other words, is she harboring a freeloader?

"I do have an expectation," Anne admits, "that Tom should earn more . . . and that you are what you earn. I think all this money stuff is a lot trickier than everyone pretends. I don't like myself for it, and I hate to admit it, but I'm less liberated than I think when it comes to what I expect financially."

They are contemplating going to a marriage counselor. Dr. Landberg agrees that openly confronting the issues, with or without outside help, is the only way to resolve them. "Sometimes," he says, "a couple will be in collusion to deny a money problem exists. It's a way of maintaining the man's fragile self-esteem. But if there's a tacit agreement *not* to confront each other, matters will only get worse."

Our interviews suggest that those couples who share an identical set of assumptions about money have fewer conflicts. Holly and Ray are such a couple. At thirty-seven, Holly is a vice-president of market research and planning at a major financial services company. Ray, thirty-six, is an artist who teaches math in the New York City school system. Holly makes $70,000 plus a bonus. Ray makes $35,000.

Unlike the other couples, Holly and Ray's situation and beliefs have not changed appreciably since they first married. They assumed Holly would earn more, although Ray's art has high-growth potential if he becomes successful. They also agree that one's worth is not tied to the amount of money one brings into the home, but by what one contributes to the total household. Thus, because Ray has more free time and is home more, he does most of the food shopping and cooking. As he says, "It's only fair."

From the beginning, Holly and Ray have put their money into one pot. Of all the couples interviewed, their financial arrangement seemed to reflect the greatest trust and respect for each other's judgment. The only conflict is about who keeps the accounts and does it better. Over the years, depending on who has the most time, they have alternated the responsibility.

(The ideal answer is that the best manager, by common consent, should handle the accounts.)

Although Ray earns far less than his wife, both agree that his income is essential to making things work. It's enough to give Ray a sense of self-worth and functions as a kind of security blanket for Holly. "If I get fired," she says, "I know we could get by on Ray's income. That's important to me."

In many ways Margaret, thirty-four, and Richard, thirty-seven, are a traditional couple: high school sweethearts; married for twelve years; eager to trade up from a one-bedroom apartment to a space that could accommodate a first child; faced with the realities of a limited budget based on a single income.

In other ways they couldn't be less conventional. Richard is an avant-garde, multi-media artist who stopped bringing home a paycheck in 1979. "Being laid off as a teacher and getting a studio grant," says Richard, "became positive turning points in my career."

For the four previous years Richard had been the sole wage

earner while Margaret went back to school and got her degree in art history. Now she is the major wage earner and performs a variety of administrative, public relations, and fund-raising functions as an officer and director of programs for the Dia Foundation, a not-for-profit group that commissions and exhibits works of contemporary artists.

Margaret, who frequently puts in twelve- to sixteen-hour days, says about her work, "It's not as much a job as it is a way of life." Much of that life revolves around socializing with museum people, other artists, and patrons.

Like many couples in their mid-thirties who have worked hard in their chosen fields, their financial expectations have risen: "We're less idealistic than we were in our twenties," Margaret admitted. "We have more material demands." At the top of the list has been a home.

They have had to compromise. Instead of the loft space they've dreamed about, they're renovating a two-family house in the Queens neighborhood where they grew up.

It's a forty-minute subway ride to Margaret's office in Tribeca. There's not enough space for a large studio, and it's not an easy location for entertaining people in the arts. But it's a good buy. "I had an opportunity to buy out my brother," Margaret explained. "Initially Richard balked. We talked about it for three months. Did we want to become landlords? Was it a good investment? How much would it cost to renovate?"

They both admit it's a calculated risk, but they now are looking forward to creating an open-plan house and, when their finances permit, raising a child in that house. They will rent out the second floor.

Will Richard contemplate a paid job if they have a child? "Right now," says Margaret without hesitation, "we're totally committed to having Richard concentrate full time on his art. My job is one where, if I had to, I could even bring the baby to work. Also, I'm hoping Richard can participate in the child care. We're extremely flexible."

Indeed, *flexibility is one of the secrets* of their success. When they were first married and each earning a wage, Margaret presided over their joint checking and savings accounts. They both agree she's better at it. But now that she has less free time, Richard balances the books, pays the bills, and goes to the bank. He also does most of the food shopping and laundry. Dinner is shared. "If we want to eat well," said Richard, "Margaret cooks."

Who carries the cash and pays the bill when they go out to dinner? "Richard," says Margaret promptly.

Their major financial crisis occurred in 1975, when they shifted from being a two-income family to relying on Richard's paycheck. According to Margaret, "It took us about a year to realize we couldn't live as well."

Both agreed that shared goals, a good friendship, a sensitivity to each other's needs, and trust were essential to making their financial relationship work.

What, then, are some of the key ingredients that make a relationship work when she is the major wage earner?

- Not being highly dependent on material things. Role reversals in which the man is an artist or intellectual tend to be more successful than those between two financially driven individuals.
- Each person must feel that he or she is making an *important* financial contribution to the relationship—no matter how small the sum. If each feels more secure with the other's contribution, a sense of common need and mutual profit is created.
- Working in noncompetitive fields.
- A man who can identify his self-esteem with his partner's. Someone who can say, as Ray did about Holly, "I'm happy when she's happy," and mean it, is less apt to be threatened by his wife's financial success or career rise.
- Partners who are sensitive to each other's feelings and wise enough to deal promptly with financial tensions in the relationship.

"In every relationship, one person will always be more

dominant than the other in terms of financial success and drive," Dr. Landberg points out. "Moreover, as couples live together and grow, disequilibrium in growth is by far the rule. The trick is to know it, accept it, confront it directly, and then resolve it."

• Finally, it helps to have a good sense of humor. One husband recalls how, when his wife's salary doubled, they agreed that she would pay for their dinners out. She then began to notice that her husband, who normally favored neighborhood ethnic places, now was making reservations at the best French and Italian restaurants in town. When she pointed this out to him, he admitted, "As long as I have to swallow my pride, it might as well be over steak bearnaise as chicken chow mein."

WHEN SHE RETURNS TO WORK

Most—though not all—of you who are returning to work are women. Whether you are returning because your children have left home, because your maternity leave has ended, or because you want to be more than a full-time homemaker, there is one certainty: When a wife also becomes a working woman/mother, the family and its finances are deeply affected.

On the plus side:
• There's another paycheck to help pay for everything from milk to the mortgage.
• If you pay someone to care for your children who are under age fifteen (fourteen or younger), you are entitled to a tax credit.
• If a husband and wife both earn income, on their joint return they can deduct 10 percent of the earned income of the lower-earning spouse up to $30,000; maximum deduction, $3,000. Any deductible contributions by the lower-earning spouse to an IRA or Keogh plan reduce by that amount the spouse's earnings for figuring the 10 percent deduction (see "Marriage and Taxes," in Chapter 5).
• If you've just recently entered the job market, you may be able

to benefit by using the income-averaging method on your joint tax return (which, in effect, spreads a year's increased income over a five-year period to lower the tax rate).

- When you derive satisfaction from your job, you not only become happier with yourself, but you often find yourself feeling less victimized by your family and more appreciative and understanding of them.

On the minus side:

- Your work skills may have atrophied and you may have lost your status in the working "pecking order" if you haven't worked for a while.
- You'll have to spend some of the salary on work-related items such as clothes, transportation, child care, lunches out, etc.
- You will have less time to comparison shop and prepare meals, so you may have to spend more on lower-quality convenience foods.
- Your salary, when added to your husband's, may, after you've used up income-averaging, cause a dramatic jump in your tax bracket, which in turn reduces what you subsequently are actually contributing to the family income.
- You may encounter resistance in your family just when you need encouragement. Your husband and children may resent not being the center of your attention any longer. You may find them reluctant to take on chores you used to do by yourself—and yet just as reluctant to lose the luxuries that your salary now makes possible.

For many women, to work or not to work is not the question: the family needs the added income and that's that. But even when the decision is hers to make, recent surveys show that women choose work over staying at home. And when your family solidly supports you, the "minuses" become minor next to the "pluses."

THE TWO-CAREER DILEMMA

You like your job. Your spouse likes his/her job. And you love one another. Everything, in fact, is fine—until one of you gets asked to transfer to another city. What do you do?

Two-career couples have three options: 1) to move; 2) to stay put; or 3) to split up (not necessarily divorce, just maintain separate households and commute between two cities). There's no one "best" option, either financially or emotionally—although there is one that's best for you as a couple.

Ahead: How to make the right choice (i.e., one that has a positive effect on your career and marriage) about relocation.

Review Your Long-term Career/Relationship Plans

Try to think three, five, or more years down the road. This can help bring the present move into perspective. Ask yourselves:

Do you want children? If so, which partner (if either) will stay home to rear them?

Is your career the most important thing in your life? Perhaps family or lifestyle—living on a farm, for instance—is more important.

Whose career—if anyone's—takes priority? Studies show that most career conflicts are resolved in favor of the career with the higher compensation. If you both feel equally committed to work, can you be flexible by thinking in terms of "turns"—this time I'll move for you, next time you move for me?

Evaluate the Ins and Outs of the Job Transfer Offer

How does the salary increase compare with the cost of living in the new location? Your raise could amount to virtually nothing if housing costs, for instance, are double.

What moving costs will the company cover? Remember, the less a company is willing to help finance a move, the more you need to weigh the potential increase in salary against the expenses involved in changing residences.

Is the move a clear-cut promotion? The higher the compensation and/or the greater the long-term potential, the easier it will be for you and your spouse to accept some sacrifice. Very simply, if you both can point to tangible benefits of the transfer (more spending money, status, etc.), you'll be more willing to weather times of stress. In reverse: If you uproot your lives for a lateral move, it will be easy to start thinking "we did all this for nothing" when the going gets rough.

Investigate What Job Opportunities Are Likely to Be Available to the Relocating Spouse

Some companies will try to employ the spouse at the new location and, if that isn't possible, will pick up the tab for job counseling and placement. In addition to any company-sponsored advice, check professional/trade journals and local classified ads; they provide specific job leads as well as indicate what skills and career backgrounds are in demand in the area. Obviously, the spouse's particular type of job or profession is critical, as is the relocation spot. A research scientist in Boston, for example, might find it hard to land a comparable job in Knoxville. On the other hand, a publicist in Des Moines might make more money and find greater opportunities in Manhattan.

While a transfer can boost both careers, in some cases the spouse may be forced to accept a lower salary, a less-than-perfect job, or even unemployment. Crucial to ask yourselves when the opportunities for the spouse look slim:

- Can we afford the spouse's salary cut?
- Is one career worth advancing at the complete expense/ squashing of the other? Remember, oversacrifice can backfire and turn into resentment and anger.
- Could unemployment be turned into a long-sought-after opportunity to go back to school, write that novel, become a consultant, etc.?

Consider the Career Consequences of Not Moving

Most career consultants agree on three things: 1) relocating is one of the best ways to leapfrog peers; 2) a move combined with a promotion is almost always an opportunity; and 3) begging off a move won't put a career in jeopardy—the first time. In other words, you (or your spouse) will probably be asked to move another time, and you can't keep turning down moves without risking damage to your career. Moral: Whatever decision you make about this move, take the time to explore what your answer will be next time. The key question here: Does the city where you presently live offer enough future opportunities to the partner who is turning down the transfer?

Look at the Long-distance Marriage Option

You're at loggerheads: One of you wants to move, the other adamantly doesn't, yet you want to stay married. So you toy with the idea of maintaining two households and commuting between cities.

First question: Can you afford the cost of two homes/rentals, the long-distance phone bills, the travel expenses?

Next question: Can you withstand the psychological strain of being separated? Most couples who successfully juggle long-distance marriages agree: It's not easy. The two biggest pitfalls: exhaustion (by the end of the work week, and after a long commute, one or both partners are too tired to put a lot of energy into the relationship) and jealousy (distance and time away can breed suspicion and slowly erode trust).

For a clue on how you'll react when separated on a regular basis, think about how you feel during temporary times apart: Do you feel relieved of some pressure/guilt about working late? Or do you feel neglected and lonely all the time? Do you stay in touch naturally, or fight about the not-frequent-enough phone calls? Do you feel confident about your relationship, or do you dwell on doubts/problems?

The bottom line: The couple that begins on firm, trusting

ground—has a history of good communication and a strong commitment to working out problems—has the best chance of overcoming the common catches in a long-distance marriage. On the flip side: The couple which splits because they both deep down think their jobs are more important than the relationship is sure to run into snags before long.

Let Making a Decision Be a Process

Chances are, as you evaluate all your options, you'll vacillate quite a lot before making a choice. Don't expect instant answers (from yourself or your partner). Instead, be aware of each other's feelings, fears, ambitions, etc. In the final analysis, as long as you both are willing to negotiate, and you both believe the relationship is worth some compromise, you'll survive your career conflicts—and perhaps even grow closer as a result.

OVERLAPPING EMPLOYEE BENEFITS

When you tie the knot, you'll probably appreciate right away many of the advantages of operating as a husband/wife team. One area you may fail to investigate, however, is overlapping employee benefits. You're struggling through those insurance forms from your company-sponsored medical plan. They seem to take forever to fill out. To make things worse, you have to complete another full set if you want to get payment from your spouse's plan.

No wonder you give up on the second set and settle for repayment from your company alone. This may be the easy way out, but does it make sense financially?

Almost surely not.

To find out, dig up the employee benefits manual you were handed your first day of work. In fact, get your spouse's as well, and study the two side by side.

It's worth it: The value of your benefits can easily equal one-fourth or more of your combined salaries. If your salaries suddenly went up by 25 percent, you'd be willing to spend some time in financial planning, so why ignore the same amount of money just because the value is not in cash?

Many of the benefits you receive are fixed, but in at least three areas you do have some options for choice and flexibility:

- savings plans;
- life insurance;
- medical and dental plans.

Unless your employer provides an unusually generous benefits package, or you're part of a cafeteria-style plan (see "Choosing Your Benefits"), you'll be able to decide for yourself the extent of your participation in these areas.

Savings Plans

- Whose plan is richer?

That is, whose plan matches funds at a higher rate? This is especially important when family resources are limited and both spouses can't afford to invest the maximum their plans allow, says Philip M. Alden, a vice-president at the management consulting firm of Towers, Perrin, Forster & Crosby.

Take the case of Richard and Nancy. They each earn about $25,000 a year, and their respective companies permit up to 6 percent of salary to be invested in a savings plan. But let's say this couple can only invest a combined total of $1,500— 6 percent of one salary. Should each spouse invest 3 percent of salary in his or her plan?

This makes sense if matching is the same for both companies. But if Nancy's company matches at a rate of 100 percent and Richard's at only 50 percent, it makes much better sense to put all the savings into Nancy's plan, where the return is potentially greater.

- Whose plan offers more variety?

Some savings plans offer investment options in three or four different stock and bond combinations. Other plans require investment in the company's own stock, period. Depending

on your own investment philosophy and the performance of
your company's plan over the years, this may be an important
consideration.

• Whose plan is more flexible?

Some companies' savings plans vest at a faster rate than
others, and some have less attractive loan and other withdrawal privileges than others. The latter may be important if,
for example, you want to use some of your savings to pay for
a child's college education down the road.

• Whose job is more stable?

Even a very attractive savings plan can lose some of its al-
lure if the long-term employment prospects for the enrolled
spouse are dim.

If, for instance, Richard's savings plan is more attractive but
he is in a high turnover company in a volatile industry, Nancy's plan may be the better bet for long-term savings.

• Is either plan more advantageous than opening an IRA on your
own?

This question arises when a couple cannot afford an IRA
and a contributory savings plan through their companies. The
ideal would be to have both.

• Does either spouse's company offer a 401(k) salary reduction
plan?

The 401(k) is a relatively new way that companies can provide savings plans and lower their employees' taxes at the same
time. If your company offers one, you should study the literature carefully to see if and how it compares with your spouse's
savings plan.

Life Insurance

• Do you really need to buy optional life insurance?

Companies may give you the option to double your coverage for an additional contribution, but if you don't need more
insurance, why buy, even if the rate is low?

A young working couple without dependents probably doesn't
need optional insurance from either spouse's company. Cou-

ples with children may want additional insurance on their own lives (though not for their dependents, say the experts) but not necessarily through an employer's plan.

- Is insurance through your employer cheaper than coverage bought on the outside?

Start by comparing your employers' rates to those available elsewhere. Does either employer provide free coverage in a basic plan? If so, that may be all you need.

You should also find out if either spouse's employer subsidizes the optional insurance in its plan. If not, chances are you'll do better buying on the outside.

If you are young, female, and a nonsmoker, you will almost always do better buying life insurance on your own, says Andrea Feshbach, a benefits consultant for Touche Ross. That's because insurance actuarial tables are still geared to the profile of a middle-aged male employee.

- How important is it for you to "ensure your insurability"?

If you and your spouse both decline contributory group life insurance now, you may need to prove good health if you decide to buy it at a later date. This is something to consider if you are planning a family and/or if you anticipate a long-term relationship with your present employer.

Medical and Dental Insurance

Some form of medical insurance is essential today, regardless of any other benefits you may choose to forego. According to the U.S. Department of Labor, 97 percent of U.S. workers in medium and large firms receive health insurance coverage through their companies.

There's no question about whether to elect medical coverage, only whether to elect one's spouse as a dependent for an additional monthly charge.

In Scenario 1, Richard and Nancy have no children. They each enroll in their respective medical plans without dependent coverage, for which they might otherwise pay from $10 to $75 a month.

They have in all likelihood made a wise decision *unless* one spouse has a generous optional plan and the other has a basic or modest plan. To decide if this is the case, you may have to put aside your pencil and paper and start using your home computer to do the calculating.

Say Richard incurs a $1,000 medical bill. His modest plan covers only $500; Nancy's generous plan pays $800. If both spouses had dependent coverage, Nancy's plan would "fill the gap" of $500 left by the other plan.

Over the course of a severe illness, this gap filling can mount up. The final decision to purchase optional dependent coverage must be weighed against its monthly cost.

In Scenario 2, Richard and Nancy have two active children. In this case, it would be worthwhile for both spouses to carry dependent coverage.

The gap-filling feature of dependent coverage works to the advantage of both parents in this case. The more children, the more cost-efficient it becomes.

Again, the final decision will depend on the cost of dependent coverage as well as the number, ages, and health of the children.

Scenario 3 doesn't exist yet, but its time is coming: Feshbach believes more companies will eventually offer the option of dependent coverage excluding the spouse.

This makes sense both for families in which two spouses are working and already covered and for single-parent households. In either case, why pay for coverage that isn't needed?

In the meantime, it's worth the effort to study the two employee manuals and sweat through the duplicate paperwork that overlapping benefits inevitably entails. The money you save is rightfully yours.

Choosing Your Benefits

With cafeteria-style benefit plans, employees have the opportunity to shape their own benefits packages. Although individual plans may differ substantially, the basic principle works like this:

You, as an employee, are given vouchers worth a certain amount of money, to exchange for a variety of types and levels of benefits.

If you are young, single, and without dependents, you may choose to "buy" an extra week's vacation and forego the option of dependent medical coverage. Or if you are nearing retirement age and your spouse has an excellent medical plan, you may opt for maximum benefit levels in the company's savings plan.

Some plans offer special benefits—like child-care credits or auto insurance premium payments—not available under normal employee benefit programs.

The importance of coordinating couples' benefits is magnified when one or both is enrolled in a cafeteria plan. Instead of planning your financial objectives in terms of what your company offers, you can work out your employee benefits in terms of what you want. It's worth spending the time to do so.

THE COUPLE THAT WORKS TOGETHER . . .

Visualize an all-in-the-family business as it would be played in a Norman Lear sitcom—the people involved basically love one another, and while you must have problems, there's nothing that can't be solved in half an hour of witty dialogue.

Ideal, of course. But it doesn't always work out that way. There are problems inherent in any business endeavor, and in a family business they can be even more intense—especially so when the relationships continue beyond 5 P.M.

Being in business with your spouse means that when you get home from the office, you never have to ask, "How was your day, dear?"—you *know*. Unless you are careful, you eat, sleep, and breathe the business with no relief. If it works, the closeness and sharing of ideas can be unbeatable; if it doesn't work out, it can become unbearable.

Maitlin Russell, of Philadelphia's Melior Group (a marketing research and consulting concern), finds that many business couples work better if each spouse has a separate area of expertise and responsibility and if they acknowledge that they can't reach a consensus on all things. He should know: His wife, Linda McAleer, is one of his three partners. They usually resolve differences by compromise. She suggests that their success is also due to the fact that they met while working together and had a business relationship predating their marriage. They share both vision and business objectives. Linda cautions that partner-spouses must not feel threatened by each other's professional competence.

Alan and Stephie Glazer have worked out a formula for a satisfying career *and* marriage by separating business responsibilities within the company and always placing their personal relationship first. Stephie Glazer is the buyer for the couple's Bedford, New York-based catalogue sales business and, according to Alan, has "the real creative flair and sense of the marketplace" to handle her end of Bedford Fair Industries well. Alan does the administering and marketing for the company and says that this illustrates a natural division of work and interests for them both, although "we often have ideas about the other's area." Debates happen between the partners, but they agree that if worst came to worst, they would drop the business for the marriage, which isn't a likely prospect.

Work-together spouses seem to be good not only for the bottom line but for the success of the relationship. Drs. Peter Wylie and Mardie Grothe, partners in the Performance Improvement Association, ran a workshop recently for married couples in business together. They say they met "some of the happiest people we've ever seen."

A family business can also be ideal for couples who want to share child-rearing chores equally. The danger is that business partner-parents can give so much time and attention to the business that the kids feel excluded.

Alan and Stephie Glazer have seen both sides of this equation since he left the corporate nine-to-five to work with his wife.

Alan says that in the beginning, the fledgling business allowed him more time with his kids. "Until the company really began to take off," he says, "I could take the phone off the hook at three o'clock and have milk and cookies with the children when they got off the bus." But success brought greater demands on both of the Glazers, and Alan admits that there have been times when his children would have liked less business discussion at the dinner table. "Only recently have the kids been interested in having input, mainly because they've both been employees of the firm in the customer relations department. Laughs Stephie, "Now *I* would like less business talk at the dinner table—especially when one of our daughters, ever sensitive to customer needs, starts to question me closely about why we ran out of stock in a particular item."

Running the Business

Salaries

If you are incorporated, your corporation can deduct "reasonable compensation" paid to people working for it. If yours is a family business, there are two conflicting temptations.

One is to pay huge salaries to family members, then deduct the salaries and let Uncle Sam pick up part of the load. (If there are two generations of family members, the game might be played a little differently: The older generation wants to set up succulent pension plans, knowing that they'll be ready to enjoy them soon, while cutting back on younger-generation salaries.) If the IRS says a salary is unreasonable, it can claim that the excessive part is really a dividend on the stockholder-employee's shares. This doesn't make much difference to the employee (salaries and dividends are taxed more or less the same way), but it makes a difference to the corporation, because salaries are deductible but dividends aren't.

The other temptation is to scrimp on salaries and pour the money back into the business, making the family members' stock more valuable. (The IRS charges a penalty tax if too much is accumulated and not enough dividends are paid.) Everybody is happy if generous dividends are paid, but there can be trouble if some relatives want dividend income now, while those in control of the business want to increase the value of the stock at the expense of current income.

Then there's the "tax-deductible allowance": The founder's high-school or college-age kids get summer jobs in the business. The corporation can deduct their salaries (as long as the pay is reasonable compensation for work the kids actually do, of course). The kids are in a low tax bracket, so they pay little or no tax on the money. In some circumstances, unemployment and Social Security taxes won't be due. Theoretically, the kids then take the salaries and pay their college tuition—a great tax-planning move.

Words of Wisdom

Herewith some tips that apply to spouses working together and family businesses in general:

- Family members must discuss openly why they want to be in the family business, what they want to get from it, what they can contribute to it, and the directions they want the business to take. They must be able to separate personal feelings, fears, and resentments from judgments about today's business problems and future plans.
- Dr. Léon Danco, president and CEO of Cleveland's Center for Family Business, strongly recommends that the family business have—and rely on—a talented and well-compensated outside board of directors to provide non-family input. The board must be kept well informed and have regular weekly or monthly meetings.
- Drs. Wylie and Grothe point out that family businesses often let a difficult situation deteriorate until retrieval is impossible. A management consultant, called in early enough, can find a way to relieve the tension without airing years of dirty linen—

or at least find a way to divide up the business among family members or make a favorable deal with an outside buyer.

- It's never too early to make plans that help the family business to operate smoothly and save taxes. For example, the business can be set up as a sole proprietorship, with one family member in charge and others as employees; as a partnership (maybe between spouses, parent and child, or siblings); a family partnership (*see below*); a "subchapter S" or "small business corporation" (a corporation with only one class of stock and fewer than 35 stockholders; this kind of corporation is entitled to certain tax advantages); or as an ordinary corporation. There are business and tax pros and cons to each form, and making the right choice is important. (If you make the *wrong* choice, it's usually not too hard to switch.)

- If the family business is organized as a partnership, it should have a well-written partnership agreement explaining the rights and duties of each partner, how new partners (for example, sons and daughters) will be added to the firm, and what happens to the partnership when a partner retires or dies.

- All corporations have articles (or certificates) of incorporation, and bylaws—legal documents that set the foundation for corporate operations and policies. These documents can be written to avoid problems: For example, by providing that conflicts be turned over to a neutral arbitrator for binding arbitration; by setting guidelines on salaries and dividends for family members; by requiring that family members offer their stock to the corporation before selling it to outsiders (so the business will stay in the family).

- Business founders must also be aware of the possibility of divorce. In most states, a married couple's property will be divided equitably on divorce—a common division is that the wife (if she was not an active business participant) gets the family home, the husband retains control of the family business. The court might also require that the wife get part of the business profits for a certain number of years or that she be given shares of stock in the business. The situation is a little different if both spouses are active participants; the business might not be able to survive without its top sales-getter or the chemist who developed eighteen lucrative patents. Some couples find that they can continue as business partners after a divorce.

 **Seven** # SPENDING MONEY

ead any advice columnist and you'll see that money problems keep them in business. Disagreements about money rank high on any list of marital woes.

Money acts as a lightning rod for other issues and trouble spots in a relationship. While you and your paramour might not see eye to eye on every financial issue, it's crucial—if you're serious about your relationship—that you discuss your financial goals and your attitudes and values about money. Figure out where you can compromise, and determine whether specific disagreements don't mask something else.

For example, if you prefer to save money to buy better merchandise later rather than cheaper merchandise right away, that reveals some important information about you. Do you know what that information is, and does your mate know too?

Perhaps you place great value on quality and are willing to wait until you can save enough for what you truly want to buy. Or maybe some hidden puritanical instinct tells you that you shouldn't have fun and shouldn't buy items (or experiences such as a honeymoon) that facilitate or provide pleasure for its own sake. Do you in fact buy what you want when you have the money, or do you constantly defer making those purchases? As you think through your attitudes, you may easily find other explanations that more closely fit your situation.

The next step will be to communicate that awareness to your partner and to urge him or her to analyze his or her own attitudes thoroughly.

Mutual respect about money matters may be tough to achieve, but the effort is amply rewarded.

MAJOR PURCHASES

You've thought that you are both tired and very much need a vacation. With considerable thought, saving, and planning, you manage to put round-trip air tickets and an itinerary for visiting Mexico's ruins in the card you have on the breakfast tray you bring her the morning of her birthday. She opens it, hugs you, and becomes morose.

For a moment, put yourself in the position of the husband whose animation over the surprise Mexican trip is doused by his wife's lack of enthusiasm.

You think you have a marvelous relationship with your wife. She's a lively, successful professional who seems always somehow to have time and self left over for you. Both you and she have been extremely pushed for the past couple of years, she building her practice and you building your business. Neither of you has taken more than a long weekend off during this time. Although you maintain your finances separately, you are each quite open about how much is coming in and who pays for what. Unlike some couples, you usually have no problems reaching agreement on expenditures.

Because you really have been putting as much as possible into making your business grow, it was somewhat of a feat for you to set aside enough money, time, and thought for this Mexican trip.

You are fascinated by the Mayan and Aztec ruins, eagerly devouring magazine articles on the subject. You have carefully timed the trip and the news of it so it would be the ideal birthday surprise. Now you are totally baffled as to why she is upset.

She, meanwhile, just feels like burying her head in the pillow. How can she tell you that she really wants a *rest*? The last thing she wants is to go dragging around dusty ruins on a whirlwind trip. She had dreamed of getting to the point where she could spend two weeks at a spa, resting, reading, and getting herself back into shape—for you to enjoy and for her to feel good about herself again.

How could you have prevented this situation?

- Have regular dream-sharing conversations. "If I had an extra $10,000, I would . . ." "If I could be anywhere I wanted to be now, I would go to . . ."
- Ask your partner about his or her needs.
- Observe what your partner is reading.
- Listen to the subjects your partner seems to enjoy bringing up with strangers.

What can be done now in this case?

The physical and psychological need for rest must be paid attention to first. Compromise by delaying the Mexican trip and helping her arrange the spa experience for perhaps ten days while you stay on the job. Then six months later go on a shorter Mexican trip, which she has helped you plan. Or if you can swing it, you go to Mexico while she's at the spa. Sometimes even lovers need a bit of space! To make it work, though, *you need to talk.*

While this particular example has to do with travel and vacations, the same principles apply to any major expenditure—particularly when combined funds are at stake. It's not a good idea to wipe out your joint savings account by buying an antique carousel or by investing in a racehorse without consulting beforehand. And as with all money matters, make sure there is no "hidden agenda" and that you really are discussing an investment—not a thinly disguised way of revenge or a momentary indulgence.

When you do sit down to talk, be prepared to compromise. Your idea of bliss is a new video camera, hers is a washer and dryer. You desperately want a BMW, he wants a Volvo station wagon. Okay, you go with the Volvo. You want red, he wants green.

Each couple has to find its own way of reaching a middle ground. Some are happy with compromising every time; some find they do better taking turns. While ways to spend money are limitless, one thing is constant: Communication is the key to better financial relationships. And communication is much easier when you're in touch with your own feelings about money and you understand your financial options.

BUYING A HOME

Buying a new home is such a major expenditure that we're giving the subject its own section. If you are contemplating buying a house, co-op, or condo with your spouse or partner, you can't afford *not* to read the tips that follow.

Deciding to Buy

You arrive home really elated at running across the perfect intown apartment in your price range at least two years ahead of when you thought you'd be able to afford to purchase a home. It has the gorgeous gourmet kitchen you've always dreamed of, a big living room with a view, and a master bedroom. The area is a little bohemian. You are ecstatic. He goes out and slams the door.

Put yourself in the place of this woman, who has spent weeks hunting for the right shelter at the right price. As a result of your husband's attitude, you find yourself crashing into a reality you don't understand. The price of the apartment is right. You know that because you and your husband have spent considerable time planning for your future finances and creating an investment strategy. You know exactly what you can spend on housing. Without saying anything to him, you've been working on this deal, which was mentioned to you a few weeks ago by a friend. If it weren't for the owners' unexpected transfer to Europe, this apartment would never have been available. How could he not appreciate what a find you have unearthed?

He, on the other hand, also knows what can be spent on housing, but instead of an apartment, he has been dreaming of buying a house in the suburbs, starting a family, and coming home to gourmet dinners after you both tuck the children into bed.

What could people do to prevent this situation from occurring?

- Before you are married, talk about whether you want children and, if so, when.
- After you are married, discuss the subject of children at least once a year.
- Continue to talk freely about the subject of children and working parents.
- Be frank about your own professional versus parenting desires.
- Write down and share your own preferred leisure-time activities (and where they would ideally take place—in urban or rural environments).
- Talk together (and separately) to couples who have raised children in radically different settings.
- Think about, read about, and communicate to each other what meaning job, children, home, and spouse have to contribute to your sense of who you are.

What can be done in this case?
Carefully analyze the in-town apartment from an investment

point of view. If the neighborhood and maintenance will not be a deterrent to your ability to sell it, then see if you can agree on the purchase—on the understanding that your commitment to remain is for up to two years only. If the apartment doesn't check out as an investment (and *you* must be very objective here), let it go, and agree to remain where you are for one year while you explore the many mutual issues this incident has raised.

The Benefits of Home Ownership

Particularly if you are buying a first home, you may have to be inventive about the kind of mortgage you obtain, resourceful about the kind of place you buy, and careful about your budget forevermore. However, home ownership is not all a matter of financial hardship. There are advantages as well.

Taxes

First, almost any home is a major tax saver. If you itemize deductions on your personal income tax form (you must itemize to get the savings), you can deduct property taxes, mortgage interest payments, certain energy-related improvements and repair costs, and even moving expenses if you must relocate because of your job. When you own a home, less of your yearly salary goes into Uncle Sam's pocket.

The Internal Revenue Service favors homeowners over renters. The two most significant ways: mortgage interest and real estate taxes—your largest home ownership expenses—can be fully offset against income when arriving at *taxable* income.

There is no comparable deduction available to a tenant for the rent paid to a landlord.

What this means is that home, condominium, or cooperative ownership may be within the means of many of you who think the cost is prohibitive.

Take the case of Bob and Ellen Smith, who are now paying $700 a month rent for their apartment. The idea of a home of their own appeals to them and they have seen one they fell in love with. The problem: They would need a $75,000 mortgage to swing the deal. A $75,000 mortgage at 12½ percent interest plus real estate taxes of $3,000 a year means a monthly expenditure of about $1,100.

Bob and Ellen have a combined annual income of about $50,000; they think the monthly outlay of $1,100 is steep. What they don't realize is that the house can be theirs for less than they are now paying to the landlord. At their income level, Bob and Ellen have a combined federal and state tax rate of about 45 percent. Since almost all of their mortgage payment and all of the real estate taxes are deductible on their income tax return, their net after-tax cost drops to about $650 a month.

Whose Name Should Be on the Title?

Whose name goes on the title is no trifling detail. In taking title you are entering a legal relationship with your co-owner which describes and circumscribes your rights as homeowners. This relationship has binding terms which affect you financially and emotionally—now and later. It's important to think through your decision thoroughly, together and with your attorney.

Compare the options—joint or single-party ownership. Try them on and see which fits your needs best. Remember, what follows are the broad outlines; there are as many variations as there are individual homebuyers. (Also see "In Whose Name Should You Own Assets" in Chapter 10.)

When the House Is "Ours"

Many homebuyers opt for *joint ownership* because putting two names on the title is a powerful, enduring symbol of shared monetary and emotional interests in the house.

Equally important, with several forms to choose from, it is flexible enough to encompass highly individualized relationship and ownership needs.

Tenancy in common works as follows:
- As tenants in common—be you spouses, friends, relatives, or business associates—you have an undivided, usually equal interest in the house (but the split can vary).

- Each tenant can freely transfer his or her share of the home by sale or will. If no valid will exists for the deceased, rules of intestacy govern the disposition.
- If you are husband and wife, no federal gift or estate taxes will be levied, but (depending on the value of your estate) you may pay state taxes.
- As unmarried tenants, only that percentage of the home's value owned by the deceased tenant will be taxed (at federal and state levels) upon transfer.
- If one tenant dies, the heir(s) can realize certain federal capital gains tax advantages if the home is sold. A real estate or estate planning lawyer can explain these to you.
- Creditors of either tenant can force a sale of your home to free up assets to meet their claims (if the equity in your home exceeds your state's homestead exemption).

Joint tenancy is similar to tenancy in common except that:
- In the event of one's death, the house passes automatically to the surviving tenant—the house's disposition is not covered under a will and therefore escapes probate (often a tedious and costly procedure).
- Joint tenancy is terminated when either tenant sells his or her share of interest in the house to a third party. This action converts the joint tenancy to a tenancy in common between the remaining original tenant and the third party.

Tenancy by the entirety is similar to Joint Tenancy except that:
- It is available only to spouses.
- Spouses share ownership of the house equally—no other splits are possible.
- The right of survivorship can be severed by divorce or mutual agreement only.
- Your home is generally safe from potential creditors (other than the federal government for income taxes) unless you've intentionally chosen this form of ownership to defraud them.
- Many states do not recognize this form of ownership. In those

that do, spouses taking title jointly are automatically considered tenants by the entirety unless another ownership preference is clearly expressed on the title.

Note: Approximately twenty states have a community property law, which affects joint ownership arrangements between spouses. If you live in such a state, be sure to explore the ramifications thoroughly with your lawyer.

When the House Is "Yours" or "Mine"

Single-party ownership differs from joint ownership in the most obvious and fundamental way—there is but one name on the title (hence one owner).

Other differences are:

- Transfer of the home upon the owner's death proceeds according to will or rules of intestacy if no valid will exists.
- If the owner of the house dies, the heir(s) can realize certain capital gains tax advantages.
- Your home is safe from potential creditors of the spouse whose name is *not* on the title—assuming no fraud against creditors is intended when you take title. (In community property states, additional precautions may be necessary to protect your home. Check with your lawyer.)

Note: Unless your state has an equitable distribution law, a spouse whose name is not on the title will have no claim on the house in the event of divorce (even if he or she contributed to its purchase). If your only reason for taking title singly is to secure the house against creditors, consider other methods of protection first. Again, explore these with a lawyer.

How to Choose

How do you know which ownership option is right for you?

Each person's situation is different and state laws are not uniform, so you should consult a real estate lawyer in your state before making a final decision. But here are some thoughts on solutions for situations outside the mainstream of the happily married couple buying its dream house. Ask your lawyer about them if you fit the scenario.

- If you're married and have children from previous marriages, taking title can be complex. Tenancy in common would allow you and your spouse to keep distinct ownership shares in the home, which you could pass on to separate heirs, but it offers no solutions to the critical questions: Will the surviving spouse retain full possession of the house during his or her lifetime? If so, who will make the mortgage payments and pay property taxes? If there is a sale, does the surviving spouse share proceeds with the deceased spouse's heirs? These, and a myriad of other details, should be discussed thoroughly with an attorney and spelled out in your will.
- Singles living together—if committed to each other—may find joint tenancy the best bet because it offers the emotional and financial security of "right of survivorship"—but it also provides an out. If the relationship sours or a career move takes one partner elsewhere, the joint tenancy can be terminated. Keeping the unforeseeable in mind, it's important to spell out differing ownership percentages clearly on the title if they exist.
- Friends or acquaintances who want the tax breaks of home ownership but can't afford to buy a home on their own could enter a tenancy in common, an arrangement that can be kept strictly businesslike. Both parties, filing separate returns, can deduct real estate taxes and mortgage interest payments reflecting their ownership percentage and share of mortgage liability.

CREDIT

Credit and Married Couples

The determining factor in granting credit is credit history.

Creditors largely judge your application on the basis of your track record of paying debts to stores, banks, and other credit-bureau members.

One measuring rod that doesn't carry any weight with creditors: cash payment of bills. Cash doesn't tell the creditor anything about how well you perform when an installment payment comes due.

In fact, without a current credit record, the odds are high that your credit applications will be denied on the grounds of "insufficient credit history."

That's why it is so important for both husband and wife to maintain individual, healthy, up-to-date credit histories. *Putting all credit obligations in one spouse's name may seem convenient, but it leaves the other spouse without a credit record in the event of death or divorce.* And that means most loans, charge cards, even some jobs, would be out of that person's reach—just at a time when he or she might really need them.

The bottom line: Keep at least one or two charge cards in each of your own names. For example, if you drive the car frequently but your spouse mostly takes the train, keep the gas charge in your name. Or if your husband/wife shops at a department store you never go to, register that card in his/her name. That ensures that both of you will have credit-obtaining capacity in the case of an unexpected event.

Most bank cards (MasterCard and VISA) do not offer joint accounts per se (i.e., accounts in which two names appear on a card and two people are equally liable for the debt). They only offer individual accounts that can have "authorized secondary users" (and your status with creditors as a "secondary user" does not carry the same clout as an account established and maintained in your own name). Your best bet: *You be the "primary" cardholder on one account, and let your partner be the "primary" on the other.*

The Pitfalls of Joining Forces

There are two potential hazards.

First, it's possible for an ex-spouse to imperil your credit history. Even though you are divorced, for example, the debts your ex-husband/wife incurred in the days when you were married can follow you into your new life. Because you were both named on the delinquent account, the bank can turn you down on the grounds that you have a bad record.

What to do: Try to supply the creditor with information that proves you were not the deadbeat. If, for example, you never used the particular card that is now causing problems, produce chits to verify that you never signed for any charges. A creditor is not obligated to give you credit under these circumstances, but the law says the creditor must at least consider this type of information.

Second, and more extreme, it's possible for your spouse to unload the burden of his/her debts entirely on you. If he/she skips town, for example, after withdrawing the $5,000 in overdraft credit you have on your joint checking account, you are responsible for paying that debt. Ditto for all joint accounts—you are liable for the full amount, not just half.

The Advantages of Joint Credit

The rewards you reap by pooling your credit arrangements:

- Savings. You slash your annual fee payments in half when you switch from separate credit cards to a shared one. (Shared accounts are generally billed at a one card rate).
- Convenience. You write half the checks (and pay half the check-writing charges) when you pay joint bills.
- Increased borrowing power. Applying for loans together allows you to list your combined income on applications, and this upped income amount increases the amount of credit you are eligible for.

The Pros and Cons in Perspective

Most couples entering a marriage aim to share a large portion of themselves while maintaining their individual integrity. The same objective should apply to matters of credit. Each partner should take advantage of the benefits of joint arrangements yet offset the potential for abuse (no matter how unlikely that seems) by demanding equal credit power.

How Credit Works

Every month, credit collection agencies receive updates on your paying habits. They in turn dispense this information to prospective creditors authorized to tap into their computer data banks.

Should you worry about what they'll find in your file?

You bet.

As any lender will tell you, it's not enough to have a strong financial statement; you also must demonstrate a willingness to repay your obligations as promised. Lenders assume you'll pay future debts much as you've paid previous obligations—and that's why you should guard your good credit name zealously.

As a result of the almighty computer, it's a snap to keep detailed credit files spanning a number of years. Creditors who subscribe to a reporting agency's service provide monthly reports on the amount outstanding on an individual's lending arrangement and its payment status—current, 30 days past due, collection account, etc.

Thus, over a number of years, a credit reporting agency will develop a fairly complete history on this particular lending arrangement—the date opened, original loan amount, current outstanding balance, maximum available credit, and a payment status report that shows the number of times the credit has been delinquent and the severity of the delinquency. If you've paid off a loan, that will show up too.

Put this together with equally complete reports from a number of other creditors and it represents a pretty accurate picture of how someone has met his or her obligations in the past. Other important information that may show up in your credit files includes tax liens, judgments, lawsuits, foreclosures, and bankruptcies, as well as a list of all companies who have requested a copy of your credit report.

Credit information may be reported to authorized subscribers up to seven years after it is first fed into the computer, with the exception of a bankruptcy, which is reported for the next ten years.

Significantly, not every loan or credit card account is reported to your credit file, an omission that can have distressing consequences. People who move to a new state are frequently denied loans by institutions that claim they have no credit history.

Why does this occur when these people have satisfactorily paid off loans in their home or neighboring states and hold several credit cards there? Because most credit-reporting agencies are regionalized. Unless you request that credit information be transferred from one place to another when you move, you may find yourself in the unenviable position of having to build your credit history all over again—no mean task, given the importance an established track record has in obtaining a new loan. Fortunately, with the ever-improving quality of computer capabilities, this is much less of a problem than it once was.

Two other reasons may account for a loan not showing up on your credit report: The lender has a policy of not reporting information about its borrowers; or the loan may be the type generally not reported.

Although you may not know it, only certain categories of credit show up in your files—bank installment loans, department store charge accounts, credit cards (but not necessarily charge cards that must be paid off in full each month), and some second-mortgage loans and leases. A loan arrangement that does not require you to repay in equal monthly installments probably would not appear on your credit report. Likewise, payment information on a first mortgage is almost never available in your credit file. Does this mean you can get away with murder on unreported loans? Hardly! Bankers have other means of checking up on these types of credit facilities.

Most bankers use reports from credit agencies as a springboard for a fuller investigation of a prospective borrower's history. After reviewing the report for obvious problems, they check to see if the credit arrangements on the report tally up with what's been listed on the financial statement the borrower has submitted. Suspicions are raised if the numbers and names don't jibe.

Another aspect that can trigger closer scrutiny is a series of inquiries from other financial institutions on a credit report. Usually this means the borrower is shopping around for credit, which could indicate trouble. For this reason, diligent bankers will often call the loan departments at banks that made inquiries to discuss the nature of the request and the ultimate decision.

One vice-president saw this effort pay off handsomely. Already concerned that his customer had requested renewal (rather than pay off his loan as promised), the loan officer ordered a current credit report, only to discover a string of new inquiries. Upon calling several of these banks, he learned that his borrower had recently obtained a substantial loan from another institution—a fact he had conveniently neglected to tell the bank. No responsible banker, presented with a borrower's deceit, would continue a lending arrangement with him.

Banks almost always rely on direct checking with other lending institutions to supplement the information available from applicant's credit files. This checking takes two forms—the verbal approach discussed above and written requests, which usually are sent out only when someone applies for a mortgage loan. You should expect to list previous banking connections when you apply for a line of credit and to have these institutions called unless you request otherwise. (If you ask that a particular bank not be called, have a good reason for doing so; bankers will assume the worst—that you're trying to hide something.) While industry-accepted standards regarding these bank-to-bank discussions prohibit disclosures that might jeopardize bank/borrower confidentiality, they are sufficiently meaty to ferret out any problems. For example, it's all right for bankers to discuss the length of a borrowing relationship and the various loans the borrower has assumed, including their approximate dollar amount, paying history, and collateral, if any. But sharing more specific details and any confidential or subjective information, such as opinions on the borrower's character, is not acceptable.

Still, bankers often warn off fellow professionals with an off-the-record word of caution and will open up even more if they know the banker calling personally. Don't kid yourself—Macy's talks to Gimbel's, and bankers swap secrets.

The key to avoiding the banker's blacklist is simply to pay your debts on time and stay within your preapproved credit limits. In other words: Exercise financial responsibility. Lenders look for credit reports with these "ideal" characteristics: no delinquencies or other derogatory information; several credit references from a variety of sources, all of which show that the borrower paid as agreed and stayed within pre-established bounds; and a several-year credit history—the longer the better. Kind words from previous banking connections win points too.

An occasional thirty-day delinquency, now brought current, shouldn't submarine your chances to get a loan, for we've all forgotten to mail a bill or lost a check in the works and lenders know this.

Check Your Credit History

More troublesome and potentially damaging are problems or errors on your credit report you may not be aware of. The ways this can happen are countless, but the situation is common enough to justify ordering a copy of your credit report every year or so as a critical safeguard—and especially when you're contemplating major financing.

If you wrote to a credit-reporting bureau for your credit history, you might be surprised to find that it has you down as Arthur W. Kane instead of Arthur P. Kane; as a VISA card delinquent instead of a VISA card holder with a zero balance.

Those errors could affect your ability to get a job; finance a house, home improvements, or a car; open an account with a department store; buy insurance; rent an apartment; and more.

If you've never inquired or haven't done so for a year, now is the time. Here's how:

- Check the Yellow Pages under "credit" or "reporting agencies" for the credit bureaus in your city, or get the names from your bank or the credit manager of a company that has granted you credit. These agencies provide a large percentage of all credit reports and cover much of the nation, including all metropolitan areas: TRW Information Services, 505 City Park Way West, Orange, CA 92667, 714-937-2000; Equifax, Inc., 1600 Peachtree St., Atlanta, GA 30309, 404-885-8000; Trans Union Credit Information, 444 N. Michigan Ave., Chicago, IL 60611, 312-645-6000.

- Call to arrange a personal or telephone interview with each bureau. You may have to send identification before a telephone interview is granted; or you'll be questioned over the phone to verify your identity.

Your right to know your credit history is guaranteed by the Fair Credit Reporting Act of 1971. It also guarantees your right to:

- Learn the name and address of the credit bureau responsible for a report that causes you to be denied credit or a job, and review your file free of charge within thirty days of the denial.
- Know the sources of information in a report (i.e., store, bank, employer, etc.).
- Get the names of all who have received reports on you within the last six months, or, within the past two years, if the report was furnished for employment reasons.
- Have incomplete or incorrect information reinvestigated by the credit bureau, and if it's found to be inaccurate or cannot be verified, have it removed from your file.
- Make certain that if an item is deleted or added to your file, the credit bureau notifies firms you name of the inaccuracies.
- Have your side of a disputed fact or story included in your file and future reports if a disagreement between you and the agency cannot be resolved.

Tips for Getting a Loan When You Have a Bad Credit Report

- Be honest: You can ruin your chances of getting a loan by failing to mention past credit problems. Your loan officer will find out anyway, and your omission will make you appear deceitful even if you have valid explanations for each delinquency. Confront the situation head on; explain the nature and extent of the derogatory information contained in your credit file as well as the circumstances that led to your problems. A legitimate explanation, freely given, will considerably soften the negative impact of a bad credit record.

- Find a banker with clout. Junior loan officers in most banks are sternly warned not to make loans to people with bad credit, an admonition most of them take seriously enough to compel them to decline automatically a loan request from anyone with credit problems, regardless of any explanation given. For your own benefit, seek out a more seasoned loan officer—vice-president or higher—who has the experience and the authority to bend the rules.

- Demonstrate that you've changed. One reason bankers rely so heavily on credit histories is that past performance is the best indicator of future actions. If you've had problems in the past, you need to convince your loan officer that you're the exception to this rule by offering tangible evidence to support your claim. Especially helpful in proving your point are copies of your latest credit card bills and copies of your cancelled checks that show you're paying as agreed and are within your credit limits. Don't hesitate to explain in detail how you've corrected the circumstances that caused you to get into trouble originally. Your ability to convince your loan officer that you've changed is critical to getting a loan.

 # Eight MANAGING MONEY

hen you were young and life was simpler, you probably didn't have to account to anyone about how you managed your money. Become romantically involved, however, and you've become financially involved. Your finances are tied up with someone else's, either directly (you're married and have joint everything) or indirectly (you're going together and one of you is always broke). I can't possibly cover everything you should know about money management in this chapter, but I can give you some pointers on financial planning for two.

INVESTING

Be forewarned: Different people have different investment personalities. Some individuals are bold and brave and willing to take risks. Others feel much more comfortable investing their money more safely.

Suppose you are a cautious investor, the type who prefers to invest in certificates of deposit, say, or government bonds. Your wife, on the other hand, prefers to invest in stocks, has bought on margin, and thinks you are too conservative. You want to make joint investments—but who's right?

You certainly have to factor personality considerations into your investment decisions, but there really is no right or wrong. It should be possible for you and your wife to find investment vehicles that can accommodate her willingness to take risks but that won't keep you up nights. The best way to find them is to educate yourselves about different kinds of investments and then to discuss thoroughly their pros and cons. Seek out those where you can find a middle ground—each of you will have to compromise, and you may have to relinquish some control over the family finances.

As a simple example, even in the stock market you can find attractive investments that won't frighten you by their degree of risk. I'm referring, of course, to blue chip stocks, but you can find others. Of course, you will want to research the company carefully—as you should any investment.

BANKING

How Much Togetherness?

It's an excellent idea for both of you to maintain individual checking and savings accounts, along with individual credit cards. In addition, you'll want joint accounts and credit, even though it will cost more and you'll have more to keep track of. Here's why: First, *each of you should have funds that you don't have to account for.* If you want to buy your husband—or yourself—a present, you won't have to explain a charge on your credit card bill or a cancelled check. Privacy is important. Second, while you don't enter a marriage expecting to get divorced or widowed, if that does happen, you'll have maintained your own credit history. You'll be spared the hassle of having to reapply. (For more on credit, see Chapter 7.)

Meanwhile, use your joint accounts and cards for household and other expenses, and for shared savings and investments.

Choosing the Right Personal Checking Account

Before opening a joint checking account, investigate your options. One arrangement may be better for you than another, depending on how the bank operates (and the rules are changing fast) and on how you operate as a couple. Consider carefully who puts what where and be sure you are prepared for such eventualities as emergencies, divorce, or death.

Are you among the millions who have the uneasy feeling that the regular checking account in which you have placed your money for years is somehow not right for you? That somehow you are missing out on earnings from interest-bearing accounts?

Others have been wondering the same thing and have rationalized their inertia with: "I don't have time to check into this"; "I'm sure it's a gimmick anyway"; or "It's too confusing to bother with."

The new checking accounts may be a prime example of everything that's good and bad about financial deregulation.

On the one hand, you have choices beyond anything that existed just a few years ago. Now larger banks may offer seven or more distinctly different types of checking accounts, and the competition among previously complacent financial institutions is to your benefit. Customers can opt for accounts with savings and loans, credit unions, stock brokerage houses, or money market and tax-exempt bond mutual funds. Instead of letting your money sit idle in a checking account, you might be able to collect interest on it.

On the other hand, deregulation has brought about tremendous confusion—and, in many cases, a proliferation of charges for checks and other once-free items.

Not all institutions offer the same array of checking services: A small local bank, for instance, is unlikely to provide the same choice of services as giants like Citibank or Bank of America. To make matters worse, financial institutions have made a science out of confusing consumers. Each type of checking account has a different name at each institution, and many sound alike but apply to totally different products. The practice is particularly prevalent at banks and savings and loans, which offer the most checking options. Be careful not to assume that one account necessarily resembles another just because the names sound alike.

There are other caveats, cautions Stephen Brobeck, executive director of the Consumer Federation of America, a Washington, D.C.-based consumer protection group.

- Watch for fees for depositing, writing, or ordering checks and making deposits. (The latter practice, while not widespread, may be made either per deposit slip or per individual check or both.) Institutions are required to disclose this information.
- Know the minimum balance needed to earn interest and to avoid charges and know the different levels for each. For example, one bank has a $500 minimum to avoid charges but a $1,000 minimum before you begin earning interest.
- Determine how balances are calculated. Some institutions pay interest (or figure charges) based on the lowest balance in your account on any *one* day during a monthly statement cycle. Others take an average balance for the month, which is considerably to your advantage. "It's easier to maintain an average balance than a minimum," Brobeck points out.

With high-yield accounts such as Super-NOWs, interest rates are several points higher than with standard interest-bearing NOW accounts. Should your balance drop below a specified minimum, you'll be paid the lower, 5¼ percent interest rate of ordinary NOW accounts. It's also wise to check on how institutions figure that balance. For example, California-based Security Pacific Bank pays 5¼ percent on its Super-NOW only for the specific days a customer's balance drops below its $2,500 minimum but adds a $10 service charge that month and charges a 30-cent-per-check fee. At competing Bank of America, there is no service charge for accounts with average monthly balances of $4,000. Under that, the service charge is just $5—but once the balance dips below $1,000, interest reverts to 5¼ percent *and remains there for the rest of the statement cycle.* On accounts with variable interest rates, check out different institutions during a single week to ensure a realistic comparison. Interest compounded daily is more valuable than interest compounded less often, since payments add to your principal faster.

Overdraft protection is another major issue. Some institutions will "draw down"—that is, pull funds from—a savings account at the same branch if you overdraw your account. Others establish a line of credit that is tapped instead, in effect loaning you funds at the prevailing interest rate. Still others draw on your VISA or MasterCard credit line, charging interest at the prevailing bank credit card rate. Most charge a fee each time you bounce a check and transfer funds to cover your account in increments of at least $50. That means a $5 overdraft will cost you interest on $50; a $51 overdraft will cost you interest charges on $100. Overdraft protection isn't necessarily available for all types of accounts at a particular institution. And virtually all types of coverage must be arranged and documented in writing, in advance. Without coverage, institutions have three options: They can pay an overdraft and waive the usual service charge; pay the overdraft and charge you for your error; or return the check unpaid *and* charge you. If you repeatedly overdraw your account, the institution will send you a warning and then close your account.

Unless you're an unusually large depositor with multiple banking relationships and/or know your banker very well, the only safe assumption is that overdrafts will cost dearly at the bank; even a merchant will often impose a fee of up to $10 for a bounced check. That means every returned check can cost $20—a good reason to have overdraft protection and/or keep careful track of your balance. For that reason, spouses may want to maintain separate accounts or establish a joint account only for household expenses—both of which are carefully maintained each month. Some institutions now impose a charge of up to $5 for deposited checks that are returned—effectively shifting responsibility to the consumer to make sure checks are valid before attempting a deposit.

Above all, investigate your options. Non-interest-bearing checking accounts may seem like a relic of the past, for example. But for someone unable to maintain minimum balance requirements for interest-bearing accounts, the non-interest option may actually be cheaper than paying extensive charges on an interest-bearing account. "Generally, be awake," advises Ellen Broadman, former counsel for government affairs at Consumers Union, in Washington, D.C. Echoes Brobeck, "There are no simple rules."

Non-interest-bearing accounts include:

Regular Checking Accounts

Regular checking accounts are offered primarily by banks. Most require a daily minimum balance of at least $500 before service charges and check fees are waived. Check printing may or may not be included. Below the minimum, institutions charge a "maintenance" or "service" fee of up to about $5, depending on the balance. Many also charge a per-debit (check or withdrawal) fee once your balance falls below the minimum.

Special Checking Accounts

In its 1984 annual survey of bank services, the American Bankers Association found two types of special checking accounts: 1) accounts with unlimited check writing for a flat monthly fee, and 2) accounts with no maintenance charges but with a per-check fee instead. Flat-fee accounts cost about $6 per month regardless of the number of checks written and are ideal for anyone with a low balance who writes fifteen or more checks monthly (the number of checks at which these accounts become economical depends on the flat fee). The per-check accounts cost about 20 cents per check. But in practice, many have a $1 monthly minimum charge even if only one or two checks are written. Individual banks add their own wrinkles, such as a credit line for overdraft protection, credit card, free traveler's checks, or senior citizen privileges.

Interest-bearing accounts include:

NOW Accounts

NOW (negotiable order of withdrawal) accounts are interest-bearing checking accounts that currently pay 5¼ percent interest. NOW accounts are offered by banks and savings and loans and have no legal minimum balance requirement. But institutions can impose their own limits for compounding interest and avoiding service charges.

Super-NOW Accounts

A follow-on to NOW accounts, Super-NOWs are also offered by banks and savings and loans. They offer unlimited check writing and market-rate interest (an average of 7.5 percent in 1984 among 50 leading banks and thrifts, according to industry newsletter *Bank Rate Monitor*). But they require a minimum $1,000 opening deposit. Interest rates fluctuate among institutions, allowing consumers to shop for the best rate. However, if an account balance falls below $1,000 (or any higher level established by the institution), interest reverts to 5¼ percent for that day or the remainder of the monthly cycle. Most institutions also impose a service charge of at least $5 that month.

Money Market Accounts

Like Super-NOWs, money market accounts (MMA) pay fluctuating rates that vary by institution. MMAs also require a $1,000 minimum balance and drop to 5¼ percent should the balance fall below that level. But higher rates of return are offset by transaction limits: MMA holders are allowed six paper transactions per monthly cycle—three of which may be checks. Beyond that there is usually a charge—as high as $7 per check. Where banks differ is in the minimum amount you can write per check and on the number of electronic fund transfers you're allowed per month.

Money Market Mutual Fund Accounts

Most money market government securities, tax-exempt money market, tax-exempt bond, and tax-exempt single-state municipal mutual funds afford check-writing privileges.

Compared to bank MMAs, they generally provide a slightly higher return, require a smaller opening amount, a lower minimum balance, and place no limit on the number of checks you draw. On the other hand, most *do* set minimums (usually $250 or $500) on the amount for which you can issue a check. Many brokerage firms offer money market funds with unlimited check writing, but the initial investment tends to be higher.

Other Interest-Bearing Accounts

Institutions can also offer variations on accounts mentioned above, such as separate-but-affiliated savings and checking accounts.

Share Drafts

Share drafts, offered exclusively by credit unions, earn their name from credit union savings accounts—called share accounts. As interest-bearing checking accounts, they are basically NOW accounts with a higher yield. Interest has no legal limit but averages a nominal rate of 5 to 6 percent, according to Howard Cosgrove, press relations manager for the Credit Union National Association, the primary trade organization. There are no minimum balance requirements, but most credit unions pay interest on the lowest daily balance during a monthly cycle, *not* the average balance. Fees are low: generally less than $2 per month regardless of balance, and most have no per-check fee. "It's traditionally the credit union philosophy to produce a product for the average consumer," explains Cosgrove. Some offer interest above a given level ($2,000–$5,000).

Unlike traditional checking accounts—where checks are returned to consumers after clearing the issuing bank—share drafts are "truncated." That means you don't get your checks back. Instead, each check is backed by a carbonless copy to provide you with a personal record (accepted by the IRS if necessary). Account holders still receive an itemized monthly statement. For people with balances up to $800, share drafts can provide higher returns than NOW accounts, and share drafts with sweep features are competitive for higher balances as well. Smaller credit unions usually do not offer share drafts. However, the majority of credit union members belong to large organizations—over 80 percent of which have share drafts available.

Multiple Assets Accounts

Multiple assets accounts have become a favorite with upscale consumers and/or anyone holding stocks, bonds, or other broker-traded investments. They are offered by brokerage firms and combine high-yield checking with money market fund investments and other features. Merrill Lynch's Cash Management Account (CMA), for example, gives consumers the choice of three money market funds: a general-purpose fund, a federally tax-exempt fund, or a government securities fund. (Returns are highest on the general fund and lowest in the tax-exempt fund. The government securities fund provides a guaranteed rate of return as its primary advantage.) Or they may opt for an insured MMA— or any combination of the four.

Customers can write an unlimited number of checks with no minimum amount or fees. They are issued a VISA card, but unlike an ordinary charge card, the VISA acts as a debit card with funds drawn directly from the CMA account—essentially a "paperless check" saving the need to write ordinary checks, but with a shorter float period. The CMA account also allows holders to borrow against the value of securities in the account and provides a detailed monthly statement wrapping up all account transactions.

Dean Witter offers a similar Active Assets Account (AAA) with an insured Super-NOW instead of the MMA option and a 13th, year-end statement summarizing tax-deductible expenses in their respective categories.

Among others providing multiple assets accounts with their own proprietary names are brokerage houses such as Shearson, Prudential-Bache, E.F. Hutton, Paine Webber, Smith Barney, Kidder Peabody, A.G. Edwards, Advest, and Charles Schwab; banks such as Citibank and Crocker; and mutual fund management companies such as Fidelity.

The primary drawbacks: both the CMA and AAA, for example, require a minimum $20,000 deposit in any combination of cash and securities to open and have $50 annual maintenance fees (considered tax deductible by brokerage firms, though not yet confirmed by the IRS).

Minimum balances and frequency of transactions are the most important factors in choosing a checking account. Following is a list of likely candidates for various kinds of checking accounts:

• Jeff is a college student living in the dormitory, where his room and board are paid in advance each semester. He earns $4,000 annually, mostly from a summer job, and writes fewer than five checks each month.

   Prescription: special checking account with no minimum balance and a per-check service charge.
• Sally is twenty-seven, a secretary, and earns $18,000 annually. She writes at least 20 checks each month and tends to live paycheck to paycheck, often draining her account to $200 or less.

   Prescription: regular checking account with a flat monthly fee.
• Tom is thirty-four, a middle manager, and earns $27,000 an-

nually. His company belongs to a major credit union, and Tom already has a share account.

Prescription: share-draft account.

- Sarah is forty-two, married, and earns $8,000 annually working part-time. Her husband, Joe, is a manager who earns $40,000. Sarah takes care of all the family finances, and Joe writes only a few checks each month. They have a joint non-interest-bearing account and stay in close touch about expenses, so the account is never overdrawn. But together they write at least 30 checks each month.

  Prescription: Super-NOW account.

- David and Jeannette, both fifty-five, are married and have separate private practices as attorneys with a combined income of $140,000. Each writes at least 20 checks monthly, has stock market investments, and requires detailed tax information at year-end.

  Prescription: separate multiple assets accounts.

Safe Deposit Boxes

Ownership

Problems may arise when married couples have joint ownership of a safety deposit box. There may be legal complications when one spouse dies. Or contents of the box, regardless to whom they belong, may be tied up if one spouse is sued, by an outsider or in divorce proceedings.

One recommended alternative is that each spouse own a separate box with the other given power of attorney to act as agent.

What You Should Put in a Box

Birth certificates, marriage licenses, divorce decrees, military discharge papers, important legal documents, and other significant personal papers. A detailed inventory, including costs, of all household furnishings, preferably with photos. Deeds, mortgages, leases, and other property records. Homeowners, auto, health, life, and other insurance policies. Stocks, bonds, and other securities.

Make photocopies or summaries for keeping elsewhere of whatever papers in your box you may need for ready reference.

You also might keep expensive jewelry, collector stamps and coins, sterling silver (wrapped in dish towels), and other valuables in your box. Make a list of these contents for home.

What Not to Put in a Box

The original of your will. This you should keep with your attorney or executor. A copy should be kept in your safety deposit box. Do not permit any well-meaning but misguided friend to advise you otherwise on this!

If regulations in your state prohibit the removal of property from a safe deposit box upon the death of a spouse, keep life insurance policies elsewhere. These policies are considered property, and both the insurance policy and a death certificate are required by the insurance company before payment to the beneficiary can be made.

STICKING TO A BUDGET

Whatever your situation, your financial plan requires a budget. Whether you love a bargain and are adept at pennypinching or are the happy-go-lucky type who never keeps a receipt, it's essential that you track income and outflow and develop a strategy for saving and spending. If you and your partner have worked out a budget together, then it's important that you both stay on track. If you are the one who has difficulty operating within a budget, you could be causing unpleasant arguments over missing dollars and goals not met.

Carol, a thirty-one-year-old wife, reveals, "When I lived by myself, my income and needs were small. Then I married and my husband had a larger income, but he also had to pay alimony and child support. We make a lot of money, but we don't budget, so we overspend. The problem is that we have no cushion. We know about the kids' expenses, but we don't expect the hole in the roof. I budgeted much better when I was poor."

Many factors create this trying and needless financial condition.

- Having no sales resistance to daily temptations. "The Pan Am 'Fly Now, Pay Later' slogan made the whole idea of credit respectable," analyzes Dr. Marvin Chotin, corporate psychologist for Blue Cross/Blue Shield. "It punctuated the introduction to a buy society rather than a save society. When we're constantly bombarded with the status of owning all kinds of material things, it's difficult to resist spending. The credit card has taken away natural obstacles—you don't actually have to have the money in your pocket to be able to buy something."
- Lacking the budgeting habit. Often this stems from childhood upbringing. You weren't taught money issues because someone else always handled them. As a grown-up, you retain the same laissez-faire attitude. Then there's the converse. You grew up in a thrifty household where Depression-generation parents rammed budgets down your throat, and you developed an aversion to dealing with money.
- Psychological attitudes keep you from proper budgeting. You may be a certain personality type. Says Dr. Chotin, "The obsessive type is a saver. The hysteric type is a spender, someone who lacks inner control and ability to plan. The oral type wants what he wants when he wants it."

    You may have low *tolerance for hassle* ("A budget will be too much work"); *fear of failure* ("I might make mistakes; I've made so many in the past"); the *charmed life syndrome* (prevalent with members of the financial community who feel "something will happen that will pull me out of the river").
- Erroneous beliefs may mark your attitude toward budgeting. Dr. Barry Lubetkin of the Institute for Behavior Therapy in New York City terms these "errors that may appear rational but are not. The victim may say, 'Only people with a little bit of money have to budget,' or the converse."
- Lacking specific financial goals. For you a budget is like a New

Year's resolution. You make it with the best of intentions, but you don't follow through. For Dr. Herbert Fensterheim, clinical associate professor at the New York Hospital–Cornell University Medical College, your problem is twofold: "1) You think in terms of generalities. You say, 'I will spend less' rather than, 'I won't go to Restaurant X.' The more specific you make the behavior you want to control, the more apt you are to control it. 2) You give up too easily. If you break the budget once, you stop trying. The trick: Know the point at which you break it and get back on it as fast as you can—just as you should with a diet."

You may fall into one or more of these categories, but *you don't have to remain there*. Budgeting is a skill you can learn. Here is a 10-point program garnered from authorities and those who have tried and succeeded.

1. *Analyze your spending behavior.* You must know your worth and the amount of your fixed expenses. Every year one publicist goes through her checkbook and figures out how much she spent in the past twelve months. She advises, "Do this, and you'll discover that you've forgotten house insurance, your annual trip to Florida to visit your parents, and your weekly budget for buying fresh flowers. I also record daily cash expenditures."

    You must also possess awareness of the details of your spending patterns. Counsels Dr. Fensterheim, "Don't be afraid to pay attention to the trivial. It adds up."

    Create a budget on paper. From your paperwork, devise a budget that works for you. Dr. Lubetkin suggests making your budget a shared family experience: "That way kids will get the input. Have a special column for the children and teach them to contribute—like a portion of profits from the paper route." Couples may want to shift the current responsibility and let the other try for budget success.

2. *Make a contract of intention with yourself that spells out how*

you want to change your spending behavior. This must be extremely specific. Instead of "I will save money," try something like, "I will brown bag it once a week instead of spending $6 for lunch at Sarge's." . . . "I will reduce the number of times I eat at expensive restaurants from twice a week to once"—and define the price of the expensive restaurants.

Write down the intention so that you can't change it inadvertently. Periodically readjust and review it. At the beginning you might keep the intervals short (like every other day) so you can adjust to realities. Then extend the periods to alternate Sunday mornings or the first of every month.

3. *Monitor yourself.* It's so easy to play head games: "I'm keeping my budget" and you're not . . . "I broke it today but that's an exception" . . . but you've been breaking it all along.

Pick one, two, or three of your savings behaviors to monitor and keep some kind of record. For example, if you spend too much for transportation and you want to cut back, keep a little index card with you and make two columns—one for when you take a taxi, the second for when you use the bus or subway. Every day mark your behavior in each column with hash marks. In that way you know when you stick to the aimed-for budget. When you have one behavior under control, start to monitor another.

4. *Examine the situation to see if you can make the unwanted act (spending money) harder to perform and the desired act (saving) easier.* For example, all his working life Marty had used a particular bank, where he knew the tellers and everyone acted friendly. He changed jobs, started to mail in deposits, and suddenly had difficulty saving. When he switched banks to one near his new office, got to know the tellers there, and was reinforced by their cordiality, Marty began to save again.

5. *Emphasize savings.* Put yourself on your own payroll. One young man actually sends himself a bill every two weeks, designed to arrive on payday. Says one woman, "I work backwards. I save first, budget later. Every January I work out how

much I'll save that year. Usually it's 10 percent of what I earn, and I try to add 10 percent more."

Try certain proven savings techniques with "free money." If you have paid off a loan, save that newly found money you would have used to make the loan payment.

6. *So that you don't feel like a second-class citizen, make psychology part of the budget.* If taking someone out to dinner will keep you from feeling like a poor relation, that must be in the budget. Make up your mind that what others consider indulgences may be necessities for you. Says one woman, "For my own peace of mind I must have flowers, wine, and cans of fancy hors d'oeuvres, but I will serve tuna salad on Limoges plates."

Play trade-off budgeting. A New York City couple loves the theater and had the choice of going to Broadway shows once in a while in grand style or regularly in not-so-grand style. They chose to stand and attend constantly.

7. *Take advantage of easy economies.* Use coupons only for things you really want—especially double coupons where the supermarket matches the manufacturer's giveaway. Go to the supermarket with a list and do not deviate from it. When friends ask what you want for a birthday present, tell them— and save the money you would have spent to buy the necessity or extravagance. When certain luxury food items are on sale, buy them and make a series of guest meals you can freeze and use later. Make it a rule to call long distance only when cheaper rates are in effect. Go on vacation at off-peak times and, even better, visit a friend in a far-off place for a vacation. Special tip: avoid auctions.

8. *Recognize your resolves with rewards.* Think of what you want as a reward, but remember you cannot give yourself anything before you perform the desired act—whether it is certain economies as starters or a certain amount in the savings account. You must make the rewards *harder and harder to earn.* For instance, initially you give yourself a reward every time you give up an expensive dinner out, then when you've given

up three, then ten. Or you can use a point system—each $10 saved earns you a point, but you must amass a certain series of points before you get your reward. Or you can use *intermittent random reinforcement*. Sometimes you earn the reward. Sometimes you don't. Decide by tossing a coin.

9. *Make budgeting fun.* Joan and Hal have a budget that effectively allows for expenses and savings. But they also have two coin boxes in which they obsessively collect small change. They walk the 60 blocks to the museum and into the boxes goes what each would have spent on bus fare. If a friend treats Joan to lunch, she adds the amount she would have spent to her box. From their box loot, in five years the couple has bought two etchings and is now working on a trip to Paris.

10. *Appreciate the fact that doing something for your good can make you feel very good about yourself.* For example, one successful young lawyer who simply could not save put himself on a training program. He monitored what he spent. Every week he eyed the growing bank account. His wife encouraged him. "Those things helped," Andy says, "but the very best reinforcer was the fact that every time I go to the bank I feel proud of myself. I know I'm in control of that aspect of my life, and it makes me feel like a winner instead of a loser."

Nine   DIVORCE

he financial complexities of a divorce are as numerous and hard-hitting as the emotional ones.

First, there are legal fees. The price for an un-
contested divorce can be as low as $150; for a di-
vorce that involves a court battle, it can be as high as $20,000.

Divorce has tax consequences. (More about divorce and taxes
in a moment.) If you are paying, alimony is tax deductible; if
you are receiving it, it must be reported as taxable income. Child
support does not have to be reported and is not deductible. In
many states, the transfer of property in "lump-sum settlements"
is not considered a gift but a sale for which you are expected to
pay capital gains tax. (That can be considerable, so know your
state's tax laws before agreeing on a property settlement.)

Health-care coverage can be affected by divorce. A wife, for example, who was covered under her husband's policy will find she is no longer covered after the divorce.

From house to holdings, from pennies to pensions, divorce affects the ownership of assets. In many states, if a couple cannot agree on the division of property, they can ask the court for an "equitable distribution" settlement. This provides for a no-fault dissolution of the marriage and distribution of assets is based on contribution to the union, rather than culpability for the divorce. The idea is that any property accumulated during the marriage should be divided so that each partner can proceed with the next phase of life without financial ties. (More about equitable distribution in a moment.)

Factors such as age and health of the couple, duration of the marriage, contribution of each to the career of the other, custody of the children, and loss of job potential are considered by the court in the division of assets. Be aware, however, that "equitable" doesn't mean "equal." What's "equitable" will often be decided solely by the judge's prejudices and predispositions.

In an increasing number of cases, equitable distribution is replacing alimony in property settlements, with temporary alimony as a bridge to support a dependent spouse until she or he can complete an education or get a job. This is becoming more common than the traditional long-term alimony.

The prevalence of divorce has resulted in an upsurge of prenuptial agreements (see "Prenuptial Agreements," in Chapter 4). An extension of prenuptial agreements is periodic inventory of assets and liabilities with the spouses agreeing to the values in writing.

The period of separation and divorce is most trying. The more you can separate the financial aspects from the emotional ones, the better off you'll be.

THE ACTUAL AND HIDDEN COSTS OF DIVORCE

Whether you're male or female, black or white, liberal or conservative, single or presently married, you must face a fact of current romantic life: There's probably a divorce in your future.

Recent statistics show that there are more than one million divorces every year in the United States, that 50 percent of all first marriages end in divorce (Texas leads other states), and that 60 percent of second marriages do too.

Behind the cold figures lie stories of pain and heartbreak, affecting the partners in two major areas: their psyche and their pocketbook.

Comments Dr. Herbert Fensterheim, clinical associate professor, Cornell University Medical College, "During divorce proceedings money can take on symbolic values. The husband may give too much. He does this to counter the unconscious image that he's doing something irresponsible or bad by getting a divorce, or to satisfy a masochistic need for self-punishment. Thus he relieves his guilt about the marital breakup.

"Or the wife may seek extra money to prove to herself that she's not helpless and powerless, to satisfy dependency needs such as the desire to be properly cared for in an infantile sense. She may act out of rage and anger and the need to strike back."

Sometimes the financial effects of divorce seem progressive. It starts small. For instance, at twenty-three, Polly split from her husband of two years. They had $700 in savings. In a simple agreement drawn up for a minimal fee by their respective lawyers, she got the $700 to buy a car. He kept the car they had. As relative newlyweds, they had little furniture. She recalls, "We walked around saying, 'I want that.' He took the sofa because I hated it. I got the kitchen table and equipment. At the time, I was making $2 an hour as a researcher. Over eighteen months he paid me $1,200 to buy furniture."

Then, on her job, Polly met Stan, a divorced surgeon. They married and she moved into his large, rambling suburban house, which he had kept in his settlement. The ex-wife lives two blocks away in a similar large, rambling house on which Stan made the down payment. Depending on her mood, Stan's ex-wife works sporadically. Stan pays "onerous" alimony and child support, all educational costs (private school, books, test costs) for his two teen children, all medical bills and health insurance, must leave half his estate to the children and must maintain an expensive life insurance policy for his ex. Last year Ph.D. candidate Polly, now thirty-three, had a stroke, leaving her with weak hands that can barely grasp a utensil. But there's no money for any household aid. "We're the divorce poor," she states bitterly.

Carol, fifty-four, a mother of three whose lawyer husband left her for a thirty-five-year-old, says, "We had a judge who doesn't believe women should get as much as men. Twenty-five years of tending children does not count. I'm not getting any of his pension. I owe $14,000 in bills. He gives me the bare minimum to live. At my age, I can't get a job in my former field of public relations. I make $200 a week as an office temp. I can't afford to take a day off to go to court. We own a co-op and we're splitting the proceeds of the sale, but I have to use my share to pay my bills. Where will I go? I fought as hard as I could. At one point I garnished his wages. My father thought this was terrible and now won't speak to me. My ex makes $110,000 a year, and I'm struggling to buy food. A woman does not have a chance against a husband who is a lawyer. I feel life is over. *I know I'll end up a bag lady.*"

Money may also make one partner refuse to grant a divorce. For years Dave led a *Captain's Paradise* existence. He had two children with his wife, then two with his mistress. During those years, the aware wife accumulated every cent she could. Now she wants to keep that painfully acquired cash and refuses Dave's pleas for divorce.

Another couple is in business together. Each always took out the same amount of salary. She saved. He squandered. Again, she refuses divorce, reasoning, "Why should he get any part of my money?"

Some Truths About Divorce Today

What new things are happening in the world of the currently divorcing?

How can you protect yourself in a divorce situation?

If you are divorced and your ex harasses, can you safeguard yourself after the fact?

Here are some answers.

Divorce gets more and more expensive. Aaron Weitz, a New York attorney, comments, "Unless you're a young couple with no kids and a very brief marriage, the cost of divorce is horrendous. Any middle-class couple with kids who splits gets caught in a terrible bind in legal fees."

This is especially true because of the equitable-distribution legislation, a comparatively new practice that exists in an overwhelming number of states. There used to be title states—that means that when you divorce, you get what's in your name. Says Weitz, "Mine stayed mine and yours stayed yours. Courts had no power to tell the spouse to transfer property to the other."

Under equitable distribution, the philosophy is that marriage is both an emotional and economic partnership. Upon the dissolution of the marriage, the partnership assets get split. Comments Weitz, "This has easily doubled the amount of work an attorney puts into a case. He has to prepare financial statements and statements of proposed distribution, search out the other's assets. I spend weeks finding out everything my client has and examining everything she knows about the other side. Overlook a $50,000 pension and you're open to a malpractice suit."

This research takes money. The lawyer must hire accountants, occasionally detectives, and appraisers to evaluate the business assets, art, antiques, and even such items as a Civil War collection of medical tools with a 42-page inventory. "A matrimonial lawyer has to be a Sotheby's," claims Harvey Sladkus, a well-known counselor.

These collateral expenses can exceed the legal fee. For example, Norman Robbins, a famous Michigan attorney and past chairman of the Family Law Section, State Bar of Michigan, needed an appraisal of a junkyard for divorce proceedings and division. The expert from New York wanted $15,000 to "just come out and take a look."

Add to that the lawyer's own cost. The retainer can run in the thousands. In Michigan, legal costs range from $75 to $200 an hour. In New York, they can run to $350 an hour or more and the cost can reach $100,000 (or much more) based on time billing. Every telephone call is included.

Adds Weitz, "Matrimonial litigation is becoming an *uncontrollable monster*. Society has got to work out an easier and less expensive way of resolving disputes without going to the courts."

As the attitudes of divorcing men and women have changed, so have those of the courts. Says Julia Perles, senior partner, Phillips, Nizer, Benjamin, Krim & Ballon, New York, and chairman of the Family Law Section, New York State Bar Association, "Men are more frightened. Women are more demanding. Formerly a woman used to say, 'I'm entitled' and could expect nothing but support. Now, under equitable distribution, she wants property." Forever-alimony seems out except in the case of a woman who has been married for thirty-five years, lacks skills, and really can't enter the job market.

Claims Norman Robbins, "In most of my cases, women's ability to support themselves has changed dramatically in the last twenty years. The courts now look on women as equals."

Robert Coulson, president of the American Arbitration Association, points out, "Today there is much less of a feeling that women need to be supported forever. Women feel that. Men feel that in general. Today women have less expectations of being kept. They expect to be helped during the child-rearing period, but want to be independent."

Even the term *alimony* has been replaced by *maintenance* or *spousal support*. Says Sladkus, "Alimony is becoming a rarity. A lawyer can take a hard line." Spousal support depends on health, age, and ability to be self-supporting. A woman may get alimony for three to five years in what is called "rehabilitative alimony," meaning until she gets the skills to earn her own living.

This new equality has not always proved a boon for women.

For instance, one sixty-two-year-old woman can no longer work. At the trial, the judge awarded her $30,000 a year for seven years. The husband makes $100,000 yearly. "What will she do at sixty-nine?" asks her lawyer. "Be like Mohammed and vanish from the earth. She will get 20 percent of his pension, but that is not worth much."

Equality works both ways. Today men also feel they're entitled to spousal support and/or a share in the wife's business.

For example, in the equitable-distribution divorce proceedings, one wife's boutique business was estimated to be worth $300,000. The judge ordered her to pay her spouse $100,000— $10,000 a year for a ten-year period.

In another instance, a Polish woman doctor came to this country as a refugee. She had to study again for her license. She married a Polish factory worker, who taught her English and thus helped her gain the license. They had two children. Then, the now-successful physician met another man and sued for divorce. The judge ordered her to pay the ex-husband, still a factory worker, $250 a week.

Divorce mediation has become a new profession. Many concur that divorce mediation is "the thing of the future." Says Robert Coulson, "Mediation is better than the courts. The discussion can help both parties to sign the agreement and to accept the finality of the divorce. If the court gives the terms, the other party can feel, 'I don't accept it.' " Mediation serves as a way of solving things without resorting to the courts, where the final divorce process can take a long time and cost a great deal. It also gives couples a sense of determining their own worth.

Coulson feels, "You can spend as much as you want to spend. How much property is involved? *Guilt takes sessions.* But trust is the name of the game. The mediator can build trust and he can warn the couple that hard times lie ahead. The wife may expect her life to continue as before. The husband may anticipate a titillating, rejuvenating lifestyle. But money will be tight. Parental responsibilities will continue." (The American Arbitration Association has twenty-six offices. For information write Coulson at A.A.A., 140 West Fifty-first St., New York, N.Y. 10020. The A.A.A. charges are low, and mediation averages four to five sessions. Or look up the Family Mediation Center in your local phone book and check out costs and success rate.)

In his book *Fighting Fair*, Coulson cites the case of divorcing couple Ron and Wendy Burton, who worked out a tight money situation. When they came for mediation, their monthly after-tax income was $2,500. Monthly fixed expenses were $1,446 (mortgage and taxes, $916; car payment, $160; credit card payments, $370). They had no cash reserve, and negotiations focused on money. The partners agreed that Wendy would have custody of the children. She wanted monthly maintenance payments of $1,250. Ron said he could afford no more than $200. At the initial session, the mediator asked them to prepare separate budgets. These were reviewed at the second meeting. Once the Burtons understood that their home was their only asset, a successful resolution became possible. They agreed to sell the house to pay debts, invest the balance, and use the income, in part, to rent an apartment for Wendy. Additionally, Ron would pay $700 a month for child support and alimony. *Through mediation, they faced reality.*

Since 1980, the Postgraduate Center for Mental Health in New York has had a divorce mediation center, where mediation counselors and lawyers work together to effect a nonacrimonious if not happy ending. The program involves only couples who are set on divorce. There's a set fee of $75 an hour to the center and, in addition, $100–$125 an hour to the lawyer when clients are ready for his services. "We're not selling cheap divorces," says Joan Lang, director of the Mediation Service and Training Program.

Like most mediators, Ms. Lang emphasizes that *mediation is ideal for the nonadversarial process.* She says, "The couples that come here are friendly. They're looking for things to work. The ties are not being broken."

Notes Coulson, "Litigation leaves scars that don't go away. It rips up lives. People are less likely to pay child support if it's been pushed down their throat by a judge."

Yet mediation is not a miracle cure. *Most professionals say the process will not work for hostile couples.* Much criticism comes from lawyers who feel today's laws demand matrimonial specialists. Some mediators have attended training institutes and are social workers; others have neither training nor background in law or psychology. Perles feels, "They can serve in child custody cases, but they're no good about money. They don't know what's fair."

The hope: that as mediation grows in popularity, state boards will set up guidelines for certifying mediators.

Judges are more open to innovative methods of child custody. For example, a child may stay with the mother Monday through Thursday night and with the father the rest of the week. The couple may live a block away from each other and the children alternate weeks with each parent. In one unique case, the ex-wife is a non-resident alien who, for tax purposes, has to stay out of the country 181 days a year. The husband kept the apartment. When she comes, he moves out. The children never move.

In relation to children, two economic factors should be considered: a) the father can't have custody when the mother needs that child support money to live on; b) with the emergence of joint custody, the divorced father can no longer get away with bachelor-type digs. Says Suzanne Prescod, editor of *Marriage and Divorce Today*, a newsletter for professionals, "Joint custody changes the pattern in terms of the nurturing male. Also, both exes need adequate apartments to entertain the children's contacts."

How to Make Your Divorce Work

Find a Good Lawyer

Do not go to a relative. You'll be much better off paying more and getting more with the additional advantage of freedom from family gossip. *Do not have the same lawyer as your spouse.*

Comments one middle-management executive, "She and I shared the same lawyer—an old family friend. He kept telling me, 'Give it to her.' And I did, thereby ruining my life financially." Remember that women seem to be shrewder in choosing a lawyer than men. Often a man will go to the same legal firm he has done business with in the past and settle for the kind of lawyer who knows how to draw up corporate contracts.

You do not need a name. You do need an expert. Says Julia Perles, "You don't have to be a famous old man to be a good lawyer. There are many sensible young men and women with know-how." Caution: You may go to a big name and think you've got him representing you. You'll speak initially with the senior partner, but he won't bother with you unless there's a convex wallet involved. He may even hand you over to a very junior lawyer.

Points out Harvey Sladkus, "Finding a good lawyer is like finding a competent physician or dentist—really by word of mouth. Maybe you know someone who got divorced and ask, 'Who did you use?' Or someone says, 'Go to my ex-wife's lawyer. He's good. He helped her take me for everything.'

"If you have no legal contacts, call bar associations. They have lists of lawyers who specialize. There is the American Academy of Matrimonial Lawyers. Call the president of your local group. He or she will try to be fair and equitable in recommendations."

Always remember that a good lawyer will cost. But if you're not in the financial middle class or big leagues, hundreds of legal aid societies exist throughout the United States.

Observe Certain Rules of the Divorcing Game

Julia Perles puts it succinctly:

- "If you're a wife, develop your own earning potential.
- Don't let the kids become a battleground.
- Try for a *fair* settlement. Try not to litigate. For a man, a fair settlement means not so little that the wife will litigate. For

the woman, not so much that the husband is left with nothing. Fairness works for both."

Exactly What Is in the Separation Agreement

The separation agreement is usually included in the divorce decree. Says Suzanne Prescod, "The separation agreement is the most important document you'll probably ever sign. You must be rational at an irrational time. What will happen in ten years if you are too lenient now? The agreement will affect your whole life and should be taken very seriously by both parties concerned."

First, you must know what *community property* and *equitable distribution* mean and which legislation your state practices. Community property (existing in eight states) is a straight 50–50 division of assets acquired since the marriage. In equitable distribution (now in forty-two states, though some question Mississippi), each case rests on separate facts, and the distribution can end up 40–60 or 30–70. It does not mean equal and does not include separate property dating from before the marriage, gifts from third parties, or property acquired through inheritance or from personal injuries. As noted previously, the cost of evaluation runs high, and you are much better off making your own division deal with your spouse.

Perles takes the viewpoint that "equitable distribution is good for women. Before July 1980, when the law was passed in New York State, a woman could, in one act of adultery, lose all support. Her assets depended on title."

Disputing this, Weitz feels that for many women, equitable distribution is "not a bargain. They thought it would be equal, but it's rare to find a 50–50 split except in a long marriage. Women can come out with less than that and the assets are not always liquid."

For many, the "emotional chattels," in the form of such concrete entities as artwork, cause more friction than working out financial details.

In one case, the divorcing husband had $1.4 million in assets. The wife was allocated $250,000—with $100,000 up front. However, the case has not been resolved because of the hassle over two paintings that together might be worth $3,000. The opposing lawyer said, "She wants the hunt scene, but if he leans hard, she'll take the wedding scene. As yet, she's still holding out for the hunt."

Robert Coulson feels these "chattels" serve as symbols. In actuality, the specific piece may be a piece of junk, but the attitude is "If she wants it, I won't let her have it." He notes, "Dogs especially produce tirades and scenes. Usually the one who feels the closest in parental feeling to the dog acquires it. One woman took her blue-chip scottie and much less support money."

In one case, the wife craved a vase that had been given to her husband as a wedding present by his aunt. The yelling stopped only when the couple walked through the courthouse door and hurled the vase onto the street!

What Women Should Ask For

In negotiating the separation agreement, women should keep certain things in mind.

Says Weitz, "Depending on age, earning potential, and length of marriage, a wife should aim for a certain amount of spousal support. But if she's getting $750,000 in assets, she won't need monthly income. *Get the assets*. Don't wait for a check every month. That's the worse kind of bondage."

Again, a good lawyer earns his fee. One surgeon with his own professional corporation had a pension profit-sharing plan worth around $600,000. The court would have awarded his wife a chunk of that—either now, or a percentage when he retired. But her lawyer never even asked for it!

It's reasonable for the wife to ask for spousal support that would terminate whenever she receives enough assets to generate income or she becomes self-supporting. The judge may say, "Let her go back to school" and expect the husband to pay for it. She should also try to get life insurance, with a clause giving the beneficiary spouse authority to obtain information periodically from the insurance company; child support; health insurance for herself, forever, and for the children "until emancipation." In addition, many women ask for and get non-insured medical and dental expenses (including orthodontia), psychiatric care, summer camps for the kids, college—even cosmetic surgery for themselves (a nose job).

A woman may try for an escalation clause. As her ex-husband's salary goes up, so does her income.

Wives feel genuinely entitled to a share in their spouse's pension. According to Norman Robbins, the theory behind this is that without the pension fund, there would have been additional salary to use in the marriage. "Today, even factory workers get a pension," he says.

Figuring the value may get complicated. For instance, a man retires. At sixty-five, he gets $2,000 a month—$24,000 a year. Ten times this—his life expectancy for 10 years—is $240,000. But he has to pay income taxes, and that reduces the total by $40,000. Also, $1 today may be worth 50 cents when he is seventy-five. That breaks down the figure to about $100,000. You need tables to show his chances of living until seventy-five. You have to hire an actuary. Maybe he'll say the actual pension is worth $30,000 and the wife should get $15,000.

Note: Women's groups are currently trying to get an act passed that would make it mandatory for a spouse to give written permission before an employee could choose a plan that would stop pension benefits on the death of the employee.

A religious Jewish wife may want to insist that her husband get a Jewish divorce, called a *get*. According to religious law, only the husband can acquire it. One man refused. Desperate to get out of this marriage and into another, his wife approached all her relatives and begged for funds. It took fifty assorted uncles, aunts, and cousins and a "bribe" of $40,000 to make the husband get the *get*.

Newest sensitive point is not who did what to whom, but who gets the co-op or condo.

In a case handled by Harvey Sladkus, the husband and wife had a rent-controlled lease. Leaving his family, the man went to California. The building went co-op and the owners sent the notice to the wife, who had been paying the rent. She sent the initial check. Discovering this, the husband also sent a check. The judge asked Sladkus (acting for the husband), "Whose name is on the lease?" Sladkus won all the way up to the highest court in New York State. The husband bought the apartment for the $79,000 insider's price, sold it for $400,000, and kept every cent.

.In another case, a couple borrowed money from the wife's parents to make the original down payment. Then the husband paid maintenance and mortgage. Who is entitled to what? In many cases, if she wants the apartment, the wife must buy her half of it at the current replacement figure.

Rent-controlled apartments can also cause fuss. In one instance, the man left the apartment and his wife for a young brunette. Then the apartment started the "going co-op" process. The wife, who hadn't a sou, signed the two-bedroom apartment over to her parents. They took title and she pays them maintenance. Now the husband refuses divorce, claiming the apartment as a marital asset. Everything is at a stalemate. Who knew the value of the apartment (then still rental) in June 1982, when they separated?

From the Man's Point of View

In the separation agreement, the man has many options open to him. If the earning capacities are reversed, he should ask for the same allocations as the wife. He must spell out custody (some judges frown on joint custody) and visitation—and later, if he fails to visit, this should in no way be considered a waiver of his privilege. Notes Sladkus, "Interspousal gifts are marital property; you get compensated." So if he gave his wife a $100,000 diamond ring after the marriage, if she wants to keep it in an equitable distribution state, he is entitled to half its current value. In extenuating circumstances, he can ask for maintenance to stop if she lives with another man in continuing circumstances. He can also insist on a geographic restriction clause; if later she decides she wants to move to Nepal with the two children, it may pave the way for better financial settlement for him.

Sometimes the husband becomes a financial victim. That occurs when he marries the boss's daughter, makes a great success of the family business, and then gets divorced.

The ramifications of this situation are many. Sometimes the ex-wife can insist the former husband stay on in the family firm so that her children will have the money she's sure he will continue to make. More frequently, the father-in-law fires him and buys back the stock or forces him to give it to the children. At forty-five, the man must start a new career.

In one case, there were three daughters and all their husbands worked in the family's wholesale produce business. Dad died, and the matriarch inherited. At that point one daughter divorced, and the domineering mother fired the husband. The man had a contract of employment, so he did get severance pay. The daughter wanted him to stay, but the mother held the purse strings. The former son-in-law retaliated by *going into the same business and succeeding!*

Acquire Some Legal and Financial Knowledge

Experts are fine, but you must understand their frame of reference. This means:

- Learn about certain cases that might prove meaningful to you. Ask friends and co-workers; visit your local law library. For instance, in New York State there is the Boden Rule. If two people made a deal and the custodial parent later says, "I want more child support," the parent has to show that the increase in the need of the child was *unforeseen.* Mrs. Boden wanted her husband to pay for college and was told she should have seen that this need would arise.
- Learn about judges. Read the local newspapers for news of who has handled what case. You want your lawyer to time the proceedings to get before the right judge—not the one who hates

either women or men. This can't be done in small towns with only one judge, but the bright lawyer can swing it in major cities.

• Even if you consider yourself a tax ignoramus, study the Tax Reform Act of 1984. This has had a tremendous effect upon many aspects of divorce settlements—alimony, property settlements, dependency exemptions, and medical expense deductions. See "Divorce and Taxes," p. 150.

Says Norman Robbins, "The onus used to be on the party giving; now it is on the party receiving." The more you know about the new tax law, the better your financial future can be. Talk to your accountant.

After the Divorce

As Yogi Berra once said, "It ain't over till it's over." When children and money are involved, the first marriage sometimes never ends, even though both parties remarry. The financial and emotional chains of the past remain. So do the consequences of the present. Two families cannot live as cheaply as one. Someone has to suffer.

The first wife must face reality. A young woman with limited earning power won't have money for baby-sitters. In her social life she's the "extra woman." Says Suzanne Prescod, "Often, work and kids become her whole life." Meanwhile Daddy remarries a successful career woman or young model and the children want to know why they can't have the luxuries Daddy has.

The first wife feels resentful. Often, she sends the children for their weekend visit to Daddy in ragged clothes, just to force him to buy new outfits. Says one second wife, "We give a huge amount in child support, but the one child comes to visit us in rags. Her shoes always need resoling and she says, 'Mummy says Daddy should get me new shoes.' "

Or the ex may deny visitation. One father was supposed to meet his nine-year-old daughter every Saturday morning in front of her home. Usually, she didn't appear, and he was left standing in the winter cold and rain. He did go to court, but the daughter, brainwashed by her mother, told him, "You're a bad man, Daddy. I don't want to see you." After years of effort, the father gave up. He says, "I have no daughter."

The Second Wife

She often stands in the middle, the forgotten woman. She has signed a special kind of marriage contract. In addition to promising to love, honor, and cherish, she has taken on her husband's guilts and financial liabilities. Is there anything she can do to protect herself when there is a hostile ex in the picture?

Says Julia Perles, "The second wife has to realize that a man who has been married before has an obligation to his ex and children or, if the ex-wife has remarried, to the children. He's got a first mortgage, and the bank has to get the interest and principal. If the second wife has any other attitude, she's sowing seeds for the disruption of the second marriage." One second wife sums up the situation bitterly: "I support him so he can support her."

However, the second wife can take certain preventive actions. She must never discuss the mother unfavorably in front of the children. She must keep all *her assets in her own name and not in a joint bank account.* She should keep records of all the extra money they spend on the children. She must not be thin-skinned (when the teen daughter hurls, "You're not my mother"). She must keep her antennae out for news of the ex-wife who remarries, does not alert the ex-husband, and thus continues to receive alimony (in one case, the husband finally heard about it and deducted the money due back to him from child support). Above all, she should remember her job is not to interfere or take charge of the problems but to support her husband emotionally. Her caring qualities are probably why he's married to her and not the former wife.

The Agreement—Is It Forever?

Usually, the agreement stands unless there is something called a "change in circumstances." Notes Aaron Weitz, "Several years after the fact, people wake up and realize they made a bad deal for themselves. Maybe they picked the wrong attorney. They try to get the agreement knocked out on the grounds that they were coerced, crazy, etc. Seven years after the divorce, one woman claimed that she was in therapy at the time and it had affected her judgment. Usually such efforts are unsuccessful. Courts don't like to change agreements."

However, a real change in circumstances can produce anything from a "trade-off" to reduction of payment. One woman's agreement prevented her from moving to another city. She wanted to live abroad. This was effected in return for a reduction in maintenance.

In another instance, a successful doctor developed kidney problems and had to undergo dialysis twice a week, resulting in huge bills. He petitioned the court and his $650 a week alimony was cut to $200, and this may go to nothing.

Separation agreements and the possible changes can be highly individual. For example, one woman succeeded in getting a clause in the separation agreement to the effect that she was entitled to lifetime maintenance. If she remarried, this was suspended for the time of the remarriage. But if she divorced the second husband, she could get it back, provided she could prove she had tried to get this from husband number two and failed. To get out of that clause, the first husband gave her a piece of property. Now she's divorcing her second husband and claiming he should pay her what the first would have done if the clause had not been changed. Both marriages were short. Both husbands have money.

Comments Norman Robbins, "Lawyers make almost as much after the divorce as during. It's like an annuity. Problems with support and living expenses keep coming up."

A successful psychiatrist and his ex-wife worked out the change in the agreement themselves. Jim took Kay to lunch. Both resented the enormous bills from their "gladiator" lawyers and Jim hated the alimony pressure. He told Kay, "Your need is now. You need to get started, to get a job." He made an offer for a one-time-only settlement. They negotiated. He upped it slightly. She agreed to the payoff of giving up her alimony.

He borrowed the money for the settlement, saying, "It made sense. Why should she be an alimony drone and why should I have that burden forever? I'd rather pay the bank. It's finite. I couldn't live the way I was going. The circumstances had changed. The money was for child support too, but my teen son was away at school and spent less than thirty days a year at home."

Jim also felt that paying the settlement made him a more ethical man. "At first I paid the alimony the day before it was due, but then I started to delay, pay a little less, anything I could do to annoy her. I've got a huge debt now, but I feel like a free man."

Enforcement of Payment

Congress has passed a new law, the Child Support Enforcement Bill, that makes it possible for garnishment of wages to obtain court-ordered delinquent child support payments.

Some states can sequester a delinquent father's property. In one instance, a man was supposed to turn over $50,000 worth of stock to be used for the support of his children. The court appointed a receiver to take over and sell the stock. In another case, a lawyer sequestered a mortgage the ex-husband held and got the payments for the wife.

As another instance, the husband, president of a corporation that he operated out of a swank apartment, was supposed to pay $500 a week in support. He didn't do it. The ex-wife's lawyer got a court order to direct the corporation to pay the amount directly to the wife.

Some states use show-cause orders. In Michigan, the court can order the man delinquent in support to appear and give reasons. As a result of his explanation, he can be put on probation or in jail.

If the ex has left town, you can hire a local lawyer in your ex-husband's new place of residence. This lawyer will enforce support. (Note: One lawyer, who insists on anonymity, comments, "Texas is great for deadbeats (runaway husbands who won't support). Texas is reluctant to enforce support."

There is always the hold-back system. Comments one tough lawyer, "If a client comes to me and says, 'He's always holding back two weeks,' I tell her to give him a hard time on visitation. The same technique works in reverse. If the ex makes visitation hard, I tell the husband, 'Don't send support.' "

Some Tricky Techniques

Because ex-spouses possess the frailty of sensitive and scorned human beings, often a certain amount of purposeful harassment and torment enter into life after divorce.

Sometimes a husband with an escalation clause in the agreement just won't tell his ex about any increases. Says Robert Coulson, "That's why it's so necessary to put an arbitration clause in the agreement; then the matter can be arbitrated."

At other times, a man will take revenge by divesting himself of any income. For example, Norman S., a marketing executive in his own business, remarried and found that his ex then became more and more greedy. His solution: He put everything in his second wife's name. He explains, "They can't touch anything Jane has. If I have money, I can have a judgment put against me. Jane owns the house. All I have now is my car. My ex is happy because she thinks I'm going hungry. If you have a first wife who's avaricious, get rid of your assets. Also, remember you never know when the first wife will become greedy."

The fury of a woman scorned can sometimes reach inhuman heights. One ex-wife refused to work and also brainwashed the three children to hate their father. The father remarried, this time happily. The ex brought a series of "I want more money" lawsuits (always unsuccessful), which culminated when she initiated a ninth, claiming she was still married to him and that her signature on a major document had been forged (the notary public at the time was her own attorney, now dead). In addition to harassment, she had another goal: to get money from him to purchase her apartment, which was then going co-op. She lost, but the ex-spouse spent thousands in legal fees.

However, the second wife had her reward. Because the decision would affect her, she was ordered to attend the trial, where she sat quietly, eyeing the ex-wife's $400 Burberry. After the judge announced his decision in the husband's favor, he muttered a few words to the husband's lawyer. The lawyer smilingly told the second wife, a writer, "The judge stressed that this material came up in Supreme Court and thus is not privileged. In other words, go write it up!"

The days of the detective walking into a motel room and snapping a picture of an adulterous couple seem to be on the wane. Says Harvey Sladkus, "Adultery is irrelevant today." But lawyers still use detectives. Claims Sladkus, "I hire detectives after the divorce; for example, in custody cases, to see if she's a fit mother. Also, if the agreement says she can't live with another man and represent herself as that man's wife, I hire a detective to get information."

In dealing with the tremendous practical and psychological difficulties in the cost of divorce, remember two points:

- Notes Sladkus, "When a woman is dumped, the defense mechanism doesn't manifest in a rational response but in revenge. Women fail to take plusses into evaluation: 'I'm young, attractive, have skills. I'm going to get over this trauma and make a new life for myself.' Instead of taking him for all he's worth, the woman will be better off asking, 'What can I do for myself?' Some don't. They have an insatiable desire to have contact with the person who left. This drives them to perpetual litigation."
- Notes Julia Perles, "People should consider a prenuptial agreement. It should contain clauses like how much the children—as yet unborn—will get in case of divorce. It should go on for maybe five to ten years—not twenty."

Sometimes the prenuptial agreement doesn't need to last

long. Alex G., who had been taken for an enormous divorce settlement, was wary of remarriage. He fell in love with Karen, a young divorcee, but feared she might not be the nice, sweet person she seemed. A worldly friend counseled Karen, "Let him know you're willing to sign a prenuptial agreement."

So Karen told Alex she would relinquish any claim on the estate if they married and subsequently separated. The wedding took place. Six months later the happy bridegroom tore up the contract.

DIVORCE AND TAXES

Be aware of the tax consequences of divorce settlements. Once a marriage is to the point where divorce is being considered, the parties are likely to show little concern for the tax problems created. But the provisions of a separation agreement can have tax consequences for many years into the future.

The allocation of payments between alimony and child support is often the subject of extended negotiations between couples who are separating.

The new tax rules relating to divorce are of vital importance to people. Clearly, and with greater justice, the IRS has defined what constitutes alimony (and how the government is going to keep tabs on it), how to treat transferred property, who takes the dependency deduction for the kids, and what to do about their medical expense deduction.

Alimony

The tax rules with regard to alimony are amazingly simple. The person paying the alimony is entitled to deduct the amount paid, while the recipient must include the same amount in income. But this simple concept takes on great complexity when you try to determine whether particular payments qualify as alimony.

The 1984 Tax Reform Act changed the rules on alimony. The new definition applies to payments under divorce agreements signed since January 1, 1985. Generally, only cash payments that are required to be paid for at least six years (unless the recipient dies sooner) can qualify as alimony. In addition, the divorce agreement must specifically state that there is no liability for payments after the death of the recipient. The rationale here is that alimony is intended to meet the support needs of the recipient. If payments are to continue beyond death, the payments are more in the nature of a property settlement than for support.

What's considered alimony? What isn't? Simple.

If a husband pays $200,000 to his wife in settlement of her marital claims, for example, this is not alimony and hence is neither deductible by him nor taxable to her. But if these payments are spread over a period of years, say $40,000 a year for five years, they take on the appearance of alimony.

A new recapture rule comes into play when property settlements are disguised as alimony. Payments of more than $10,000 per year are deductible as alimony only if they are required to be made in each of six straight years (beginning with the year in which payments are first made). Thus, in the above example, calling for payments over five years, only $10,000 a year would be treated as alimony.

Moreover, if payments for a given year are deductible but in a later year there is a decrease of more than $10,000, part of the earlier year's alimony is recaptured; i.e., is taxable income to the payer and deductible by the recipient.

This provision can produce adverse results for both parties because the recapture is reflected on the later year's return. Take the case of Frank and Ann, who are divorced. Frank's income is $100,000 a year; Ann has no income of her own. Frank agrees to pay "alimony" for 10 years; $50,000 in Year 1 and $10,000 a year for each of the next nine years. Because the $50,000 paid in Year 1 is deductible by Frank and income to Ann, each of them winds up paying tax on $50,000.

In Year 2, Frank pays $10,000, with the result that $30,000 is recaptured [$50,000 less $10,000 (paid) less $10,000 (safety zone)]. Frank winds up with $130,000 income for Year 2. Ann is entitled to a $30,000 deduction, but with only $10,000 of income against which to offset it, most of it is wasted. The only winner here is the tax collector.

It's not clear if Congress intended such a result. Don't be surprised if Congress takes another look at this provision and changes the rules again.

There's a new break for nonworking recipients of alimony when it comes to retirement planning. A working person can contribute and deduct up to $2,000 a year to an Individual Retirement Account (IRA). The definition of compensation for IRA purposes has been expanded to include alimony.

In the past, if a recipient of alimony was working, the compensation received could be the basis for an IRA contribution. But a nonworking alimony recipient was generally barred from putting any funds into an IRA. Under the new definition, starting in 1985, an individual with only alimony income can also set aside up to $2,000 a year in an IRA.

Property Settlements

Finally. Some common sense with regard to property settlements.

Let's look at a not unusual situation. John and Mary have been having marital problems for some time and have finally decided to split up. Through her attorney, Mary has demanded that John turn over to her the title to their home that is currently in John's name. In addition, she wants some land (also in John's name) that they bought several years ago as an investment.

The home, which is now worth $150,000, cost $60,000. The land was purchased for $20,000 and is now worth $100,000.

Until now, if John agreed to give Mary what she asked for, he would have been reeling from being taxed on $170,000 of gain. To add insult to injury, Mary's basis (cost for tax purposes) for these assets is their value at the time she receives them. Thus, if a year later Mary sold the investment property for $115,000, she would be taxed on a gain of only $15,000.

The new law seeks a more "equitable" result. A spouse who transfers property incident to a divorce is relieved of the tax on the gain. But the trade-off is that when the spouse who receives the property sells it, he or she will have to pay tax on the *full* appreciation. Thus, in the above example, when Mary sells the property for $115,000, she gets hit with the tax on a gain of $95,000 (based on the original cost of $20,000).

Dependency Exemptions

Although both parents may be contributing to the support of their children, only one is entitled to claim dependency exemptions for them. Generally, the parent with custody of the child is entitled to the exemption (worth the equivalent of a $1,000 deduction per child).

There was an exception under prior law under which the noncustodial parent was entitled to the exemption if he or she provided more for the support of the child than did the custodial parent. However, the noncustodial parent generally has no way to know exactly how much support is provided by the custodial parent. Because of this uncertainty, the noncustodial parent would often claim a dependency exemption in cases where the custodial parent was also claiming an exemption for the same child.

This left the tax collector in the middle. Obviously, one of the parents was entitled to the exemption, but determining which one was a difficult task. When faced with this situation, Internal Revenue agents generally would disallow the deduction for both parents and force them to go to court to try to resolve who in fact provided more support.

The new law seeks to avoid this dilemma. It retains the general rule that the custodial parent is entitled to the exemption. But the noncustodial parent can no longer (effective starting in 1985) claim an exemption based on support payments. Instead, the noncustodial parent gets the exemption only if the custodial parent releases his or her claim to the exemption. The custodial parent can sign a written statement promising not to claim the child as a dependent for the year. The noncustodial parent claiming the child must attach this statement to his or her return.

Although the waiver statement can be for several specified years or permanent, prudence would seem to dictate that a new statement be furnished at the end of each year. This is one way to ensure that future support payments will, in fact, be paid.

Handling the Medical Expense Deduction

One provision of the new law enables many divorced parents to arrange for the payment of their children's medical expenses in such a way as to cut their tax bill. Normally, medical expenses are deductible only if paid for a dependent. In the case of divorced parents, the law now treats the children as dependents of both parents for purposes of the medical expense deduction. Because medical expenses are deductible only to the extent they exceed 5 percent of adjusted gross income, medical payments can be shifted between the parents to maximize the deduction.

Example: Under their divorce arrangements, Dave and Helen have agreed that Dave will be responsible for all medical and dental expenses for their daughter, Lisa. Lisa is having orthodontia at a cost of $3,000. Dave's adjusted gross income is $60,000; Helen's is $20,000.

Assuming there are no other medical expenses for the year, Dave would get no tax deduction if he paid the $3,000. (The expense doesn't exceed 5 percent of $60,000.) But if instead Dave gives Helen the $3,000 and she in turn pays the orthodontist, she gets a medical deduction of $2,000 ($3,000 less 5 percent of $20,000).

IRS and Alimony

Simply because you are paying and claiming a deduction for alimony is no reason to be overly concerned about Internal Revenue checking up on you. The tax people don't ask you to attach a copy of your divorce agreement to your return, but the tax collector has a new tool to help it keep tabs on a divorced couple's alimony arrangements.

Starting with 1985 returns (i.e., those that will be filed in 1986), anyone paying alimony and taking a deduction for it will have to identify the recipient (including Social Security number) on his return. Failure to do so will trigger a $50 penalty.

Tax-Motivated Divorce

Tax-motivated sham divorce won't be recognized. Don't follow the lead of one enterprising couple. They came up with an interesting way to avoid the marriage penalty tax. To use the more advantageous single person's rate schedule, the couple got a Haitian divorce during a vacation at year's end. Upon their return to the U.S. early the next year, they remarried. This process was repeated a year later.

The IRS and the courts say the "sham transaction doctrine" can be applied if the couple, at the time the divorce was obtained, fully intended to remarry. Applying that doctrine, the divorce is not recognized and the couple are treated as married.

But the IRS, in a private letter ruling, has indicated that it's okay for a couple to get a divorce but continue to live together. As long as their intent was to stay divorced, they will be treated as unmarried.

Legal Fees

Bear in mind that the tax implications of a marital split are far-reaching and begin well before the divorce is finalized.

For example, legal fees *specifically for tax advice or research* in connection with a divorce, separation, or property settlement may be taken as an itemized deduction. In addition, legal fees for matters such as child custody—a complex legal issue with *some* tax implications—may be deducted. In each case the charge for the tax work must be specific, i.e., show the time and charges related to tax matters separately from other charges.

Legal fees incurred to *obtain* taxable alimony may be deducted, although fees incurred in an effort to *resist* alimony payments are nondeductible.

No deduction is allowed for payment of your spouse's legal fees. The deduction is allowed only for advice on your own tax problems.

DIVORCE AND PENSIONS

Recently, a woman in Washington, D.C., spent $20,000 in legal fees for a complicated and painful divorce. Shortly before she was to sign the property settlement, a friend asked whether her lawyer had tried to obtain part of her soon-to-be ex-husband's pension. She had her lawyer investigate and he secured 50 percent of the pension—*just in time*.

Her situation, perhaps more costly than most, is all too typical. Retirement is probably an experience not even considered during divorce, but it must not be ignored before signing the divorce settlement.

In many marriages, the working spouse's pension ranks as the couple's most valuable unmortgaged asset. When a couple in which the wife has raised the children and maintained the home splits up, divorce can swamp her financial future. And even wives who hold paying jobs outside the home may not have accumulated retirement benefits through their jobs. Moreover, since pensions are based on earnings, women's pensions almost invariably amount to less than those of most men. Men rarely find themselves in this predicament; as a rule, it's divorced wives who should explore these issues thoroughly.

"Any woman who depended on her husband's earnings during marriage will depend on them during retirement," says Anne Moss, a lawyer at the Pension Rights Center and co-author of the book *Your Pension Rights at Divorce*. "If divorce seems likely, the time to check out pension benefits is before the divorce takes place."

The key to achieving part of the pension lies in choosing an experienced, knowledgeable lawyer. Pension issues do not form part of mainstream domestic relations law, which is the divorce lawyer's bailiwick, and those relevant laws not buried in the tax code are obscure or new.

"This is essentially an undeveloped area of law," notes Anne Moss.

Because of a California Supreme Court decision in 1975, an attorney who fails to seek profit-sharing or pension benefits in divorce could be liable for malpractice. Many lawyers are paying attention to and have learned about the statutes in their states. Karen Friedman, also at the Pension Rights Center, advises women to interview prospective lawyers carefully, ask about applicable state laws regarding pensions, and determine whether they've had experience dealing with this issue. "Interview several lawyers before selecting one," she counsels. "Don't assume a lawyer will know to ask about pensions. Many of them still don't do it."

Most states now consider a husband's retirement benefits to be part of the marital property, and in most states, pensions can be divided. Courts in community property states generally view pensions as community property, acquired during the marriage and belonging to both spouses. Arizona, California, Idaho, Louisiana, Texas, Nevada, New Mexico, and Washington are community property states.

Two states don't divide pensions, as a rule. These are Mississippi and West Virginia, where property belongs to the spouse with "title," that is, whose name is on the ownership certificate.

The remaining forty states and the District of Columbia divide marital assets equitably, regardless of whose name is on the title. At least half of these treat pensions as joint marital property and view pensions as divisible assets. The courts weigh a number of factors when determining how to divide property fairly, including the length of the marriage, income of each spouse, and each spouse's contributions to the marriage.

But just because a state divides pensions doesn't mean the courts will do so in every case. For example, if the husband is not yet vested (guaranteed benefits) in a pension plan, the wife's chances of sharing it diminish.

Moreover, in some situations, federal law supersedes state law in the matter of pensions and determines whether and how to split a pension.

In addition, courts might not divide pensions of younger couples in which both spouses work.

Even if the wife wins a share of the pension, she may have the option of accepting marital property of equal value instead. In situations where she wants to sever all ties with her former husband or if she's concerned about his health or if retirement is still decades away, this can be a sensible option. Since accepting other property can have tax consequences, a lawyer or accountant should review the decision before it's made final.

In virtually all cases, however, it's to the wife's advantage to have the pension considered marital property. Once it's divided, her share can't be taken away, unlike alimony and child support, which are contingent on circumstances.

Development of this area of law is bound to increase and speed up, and the past few years have seen a number of key changes affecting millions of men and women. A review follows:

- The 1983 Defense Authorization Act gave the states the right to decide whether a military pension is marital property. Military wives divorced in or after February 1983 can take advantage of this law, and if awarded part of the husband's pension, a military wife can receive her share directly, as long as the marriage lasted at least ten years of the husband's military service.

   Military wives divorced before February 1983 who did not receive a share of their husbands' pensions should consult with a lawyer. In some circumstances, according to this new law, they might be able to return to court and obtain a change in the original decision.

   The law applies to pensions paid by all branches of the military, including the coast guard, but does not cover pensions paid by the Veterans Administration.
- The financial futures of ex-spouses of foreign service officers

are now protected by a 1980 law that provides up to 50 percent of retirement benefits if the couple was married ten or more years and divorced on or after February 15, 1981. Even if the marriage lasted less than ten years, a wife can share the pension if her husband agrees or if the court awards it to her. Divorced spouses are automatically entitled to pension benefits as long as the marriage lasted ten years.

- In civil service pensions, the courts can decide whether to divide federal civil service pensions. The courts also can order the U.S. Office of Personnel Management to pay the pension share directly to the divorced spouse. In contrast, state and local government pensions generally lack special provisions for divorced spouses. Since federal laws leave these alone, for the most part, division of pensions is left to the courts.
- In many ways, private pension plans are the most problematic when it comes to divorce. ERISA, the Employee Retirement Income Security Act of 1974, leaves unanswered many questions regarding pensions and divorce, even though it was never intended to deny part of a pension to an ex-spouse. The courts are more and more inclined to hold that ERISA's purpose is to provide adequately for both the employee and the spouse. It seems likely that the most significant changes affecting pensions and divorce will occur in pensions covered by ERISA.

For a copy of *Your Pension Rights at Divorce: What Women Need to Know*, send $2 to the Women's Pension Project, 1346 Connecticut Ave., N.W., Suite 932, Box S-3, Washington, D.C. 20036.

DIVORCE AND SOCIAL SECURITY

Three years ago Alice King, a sixty-year-old housewife, joined the ranks of displaced homemakers—after thirty-eight years of marriage. In the divorce settlement her ex-husband, Arthur, agreed to pay $800 a month in alimony and deeded the house now worth about $100,000, to her. Six years remain on the mortgage, on which she makes monthly payments of $345. She also kept one of their cars.

But the upkeep on the house, repairs, utilities, and other maintenance costs exceeded her expectations, and as the months passed, the bills piled up.

Alice found a part-time job, and her take-home pay of $75 a week helped some. But one night her car broke down, and the expensive repairs needed to fix it made Alice realize that she still needed additional income.

A friend then suggested that she find out whether she could get Social Security benefits.

It was a pleasant surprise to her to find that it is now possible for a divorced spouse to qualify for benefits based on the ex-spouse's earnings record—even if that spouse is still working.

Under the law as it stood before January 1985, benefits could not be paid to a divorced wife until her former husband applied for his retirement benefits. And if he returned to work after becoming entitled to benefits and in his new job earned a substantial income, her benefit checks could be suspended.

Beginning January 1985, however, a divorced spouse sixty-two or over can collect his or her benefits even if the ex-spouse hasn't applied, so long as he or she is otherwise eligible to collect Social Security and the couple has been divorced at least two years. That latter provision was designed to discourage couples from divorcing solely to enable a dependent spouse to collect benefits while the other was not really retired.

Even though Arthur continues to work, Alice is eligible for a divorced wife's benefit, calculated by taking half of Arthur's basic retirement benefit (his PIA or Primary Insurance Account) of $700, and then reducing that one half by 25/36ths of 1 percent for every month that she is shy of age sixty-five before her benefits start—six months, in her case. Alice's monthly benefit will amount to about $335.

Except for this new provision and the requirement that the marriage has lasted at least ten years, the qualifications for a divorced wife or widow to receive benefits are much the same as for non-divorced spouses.

The current requirements represent a considerable liberalization of earlier provisions. Until a 1977 change in the law, a marriage of at least twenty years' duration was a prerequisite for collecting benefits as a divorced wife or widow. But beginning with the month of January 1979, these benefits became payable after at least ten years of marriage to those divorced in 1979 and later, and also, retroactively, to those divorced earlier.

The 1983 amendments also changed the law to reflect court decisions requiring Social Security benefits to be paid to divorced husbands and surviving divorced widowers under the same conditions as to divorced wives and widows. So-called "gender distinctions" have been eliminated. Thus, fathers who take on the care of children following divorce have the same Social Security protection long afforded divorced mothers.

A divorced mother or father who cares for children under age sixteen or over sixteen but disabled is eligible for monthly mother's or father's benefits in the following situations (note that a marriage need not have lasted at least ten years in situations in which payments are made to the divorced person as a caretaker of the children):

1) if the divorced wage-earning spouse dies;
2) if the divorced wage-earning spouse is severely disabled and is expected to remain so for at least twelve months, or indefinitely;
3) if the wage-earning spouse retires.

Incidentally, these benefits are payable regardless of how many times the wage earner has married and how many other beneficiaries may also be eligible for payments based on the same record of earnings.

The benefits payable to divorced spouses are not deducted from their former spouses' checks. These are separate benefits, equal to no more than half the amount the ex-spouse receives.

And when the former spouse dies, the surviving ex-spouse is entitled to widow's (or widower's) benefits as early as age sixty, or age fifty in case of severe disability.

Meanwhile, should your former spouse remarry, you remain eligible for your Social Security benefit as a divorced spouse. If *you* should remarry while your former husband is still living, your benefits as a spouse would stop. However, should your ex-spouse be deceased at the time of your remarriage, your benefits would continue, providing you are sixty or over at that time (or fifty to fifty-nine but disabled).

Thus, if and as your family relationships change, it's a good idea to call or ask your Social Security office how the change may affect present or future payment of benefits.

Ten   DEATH

eath is not a happy subject, but it is a fact of life and best treated realistically. Obviously, your death would affect your loved one(s)—both emotionally and financially—and the death of your partner would affect you. Ahead: How to make your own will and funeral arrangements and how to deal with the death of a spouse.

WILLS AND FUNERAL ARRANGEMENTS

Planning Ahead

Planning for your death may not appeal to you, but it is one of the most considerate and mature things you can do for your family.

A will is a must. Without one, you have absolutely no con-

163

trol over how your property will be distributed. Your assets may become the target of taxes. Most important, you place your family in a tense, uncertain, and potentially divisive situation.

To provide and protect is the purpose of your will, so be sure it:

- allows for clear, easy distribution of assets and liquidity;
- guarantees assets will be properly managed;
- assures reasonable continuation of your family's lifestyle;
- minimizes or eliminates the burden of taxes.

If you are married, both you and your spouse should have wills.

You should own a family cemetery plot if you request burial in your will. Make sure you see the cemetery and the plot before you buy. Be careful about the contract's stipulations as to installment payments.

Another must: prearranged funeral services for burial or cremation. They will not only spare your bereaved family the effort and complication of making arrangements; they will shield them from making hasty and costly decisions. The average cost of a funeral is a shocking $2,000.

A memorial society can make preplanning easy. These societies provide specific local information on funeral services, burial, cremation, and plots, with details on how much they cost. For more information, send a self-addressed envelope to the Continental Association of Funeral and Memorial Societies, 1828 L Street, N.W., Washington, D.C. 20036. In Canada, write to the Memorial Society Association of Canada, Box 96, Station A, Weston, Ontario M9N 3M6.

If you decide to pay for funeral arrangements in advance, be sure that the money is placed in a special savings account so you, *not* the funeral director, collect the interest.

And before buying a funeral package or cemetery plot, find out what arrangements can be made if you move. Many cemeteries belong to a nationwide lot-exchange program that allows individuals to trade plots in different areas.

Of Wills and Probate

In the late sixties, a friend of mine was named executor of his father's estate. The first thing he did in that capacity was something almost unheard of at the time. He got in touch with a lawyer who was a friend of his and asked him what he would charge to process the will through probate.

The lawyer, who had an excellent practice, gave him a detailed written estimate based on his hourly fee. The price wasn't all that low, but it was half the 5 percent standard fee lawyers in that area were then charging. Prior to 1977, lawyers couldn't advertise, so there was really no competition and fees tended to be fixed.

My friend then went to the lawyer who had drawn up his father's will, a member of a prestigious, old-line firm, and asked him what he would charge.

"Oh, the usual fee," was the almost too casual reply.

My friend took out the estimate the first lawyer had given him. "If you don't meet that price," he said, "you don't get the business."

After great protestations of shock and indignation that anyone would even think "the usual fee" was negotiable, the lawyer cut his price to meet the estimate.

Times have changed.

That story triggered a memory of something similar that had happened to another friend of mine.

A few years ago, my friend's mother died and left a modest estate, naming her three children as both executors and heirs. This created friction and, to complicate it still further, my friend and her husband were living in a different city.

My friend's husband thought her interests were not being properly protected, so he got a lawyer. He had no experience in dealing with lawyers, so he engaged a friend of a friend, a young graduate of Harvard Law School, whom he also knew slightly.

Although there was a specific point at issue—namely, how two properties which were left in joint names were to be disposed of—the lawyer told my friend's husband he would only take the case for the "required" fee of 5 percent. This was not only 5 percent of my friend's portion, but 5 percent of the other heirs' portions too, who would have to get their own lawyers and pay a similar charge.

My friend and her husband wound up paying $1,500 for less than a half day's work, and so did the other heirs.

Like almost all first-time clients, my friend and her husband had no idea that they had the prerogative—in fact, the responsibility—of hiring the lawyer to work for them in a way that they wanted and needed. They had committed the classic blunder in hiring a lawyer: They had let him define the conditions and set the terms.

Because of this, they spent more money than they had to and created even more friction.

For legal help and advice, they could have gone to HALT. HALT (Help Abolish Legal Tyranny) is a consumer-advocate organization. From just an idea, a single desk, and no money, it has grown in less than seven years to almost 140,000 members. When David Scull, a Maryland lawyer on the board of directors of HALT, appeared on the Phil Donahue show with a HALT staff member, it produced a flood of applications for membership. (Dues are nominal—a membership contribution is $15. Write to HALT, 201 Massachusetts Ave., N.E., Washington, D.C. 20002.)

Two of the manuals HALT publishes, *Probate* and *Shopping for a Lawyer*, answer many questions on estate planning.

The probate manual is a must for executors, administrators, or personal representatives (the term that's coming into more general use). It includes a complete itemized checklist that applies, with only slight variations, to the probate procedures of all fifty states. The publication is written to guide personal representatives through probate on their own, or at least to help them with enough of it so that lawyers' charges are minimized.

The pamphlet contains chapters on the will, the personal representative, estate administration, estate inventory, estate claims, real estate sales, non-probate property transfers, taxes, probate fees, closing the estate, and distributing the assets, plus appendices with state-by-state detail on state rules, laws of intestacy, taxes, and spouses' right of election.

The other manual from HALT, *Shopping for a Lawyer*, covers questions such as whether you need a lawyer, shopping around, interviewing lawyers, fees, making the final choice, and making arrangements with the lawyer you select. There's even a sample contract to employ the attorney.

By consulting several of the manuals and books listed in the bibliography, you can uncover even more useful information.

The IRS has two very useful publications—Publication 559 (revised November 1983), *Tax Information for Survivors, Executors, and Administrators*, and Publication 448, *Federal Estate and Gift Taxes*.

Tax Information for Survivors, Executors, and Administrators takes you step-by-step through the tax obligations of the deceased and the estate and includes illustrations of all the necessary forms, with due dates. Not all these are necessary in every case. They just cover all possible situations.

Federal Estate and Gift Taxes has fifty-six pages of detailed explanation, with examples. It's not that easy to follow, but by reading it you'll know what an estate planner is talking about if you need to hire one. They can often save you several times their fees in reduced tax liability.

For example, George Forde, chairman of the probate section of the Philadelphia Bar Association, described how federal taxes connected with inheritance could be deferred or eased. By staggering the fiscal years for the estate itself and for the different trusts you could create for the estate (which you might want to do if there's a large amount of money involved), tax payments could be put forward into succeeding years or even reduced by adjusting income and estate taxes to best advantage.

"By timing the distributions," he said, "you wouldn't actually feel the pinch until two or three years later."

Of course, you'd need someone who would know how to do

that unless you were unusually proficient at interpreting the tax regulations yourself.

Probates are getting simpler. In 1971, Idaho became the first state to adopt the Uniform Probate Code (UPC). That law, drafted in large part by Richard V. Wellman, professor at the University of Georgia Law School, greatly simplifies probate procedures. In the first full year of its operation, it reduced average probate fees Idaho attorneys charged from 3.5 percent of the gross estate to 1.8 percent—just about half. Fourteen other states have adopted that law entirely, or its principal provisions, but the benefits have, in large measure, been retained by the probate lawyers, who are getting the same high fees for a lot less work. For instance, Pennsylvania is considered a UPC state, yet its probate fees, according to HALT's probate manual, are among the highest in the country—as high as 7 percent in Philadelphia.

There is a way to lower costs. The state of Wisconsin has the final answer to inflated probate costs. In 1973 it passed the Informal Administration of Probate law, making it possible to probate an estate without an attorney. The procedure is so simple that a very large percentage of estates are handled that way with or without a will. As a result, the probate fees of many attorneys in Wisconsin are now as little as $500.

Scull, who specializes in probate, says that the Maryland probate code is so simple that he has been able to shave the going rate as much as 90 percent. Scull encourages the personal representatives to do the busywork themselves—running around to banks and other similar errands. For 10 to 20 hours work, which Scull says is all it usually takes, his average fees range between $1,500 and $3,500.

But lawyers have shown extreme reluctance to reduce their fees accordingly. The courts haven't helped because, says Scull, judges are elected. "The courthouse officials' basic constituency is the bar association, and they're not looking for a fight," he explained.

Even if you are not of an age where planning your own estate seems like something you ought to know, you may have parents or other older relatives. That means you might be appointed a personal representative sooner than you think. Or you may be a single parent with minor children and want to provide all the safeguards you can.

Not only can you shop for a lawyer when you make a will, but your shopping should include estimated charges for probate. Your assets will change over time, and your will may need to be updated, but knowing what the charges will be and who will handle them is, in the best sense, protecting your assets.

According to David Smilk, a lawyer in suburban Philadelphia who specializes in estate planning, you can even make a contract with your executor for a fixed fee that will be valid after your death. If all your heirs are minors and you have a sizable estate, that's something you might want to consider. Smilk emphasized that the lawyer who drew up the will should *not*, because of the conflict of interest, be appointed executor of the estate.

One more reason to shop around: There are 650,000 lawyers now, 450,000 of whom are in private practice. They are not all in top-notch firms. As George Forde, chairman of the probate section of the Philadelphia Bar Association told us, the large firms hire fewer than 10 percent of all law school graduates. That leaves a hefty number of other lawyers anxious for your business. A little comparative shopping and a little negotiation of fee could save your heirs grand sums.

DEATH OF A SPOUSE

What to Do

When there's a death in the family, among many things you, as the surviving spouse or relative, must take care to:

- obtain certified copies of the death certificate;

- get the original copy of the will;
- notify the deceased's lawyer, insurance agents, and accountant;
- contact your local Social Security office to inform it of the death and to determine your eligibility for death or survivor benefits;
- search for stocks, bonds, savings certificates, passbooks, ownership deeds, and the like so you can create an inventory for estate purposes;
- inform banks, brokerage houses, and other firms where the deceased had accounts, debts, loans, etc.
- notify the deceased's employer and business associates and find out about death or any other benefits;
- if applicable, inform the Veterans Administration or other organizations regarding death benefits;
- file an income tax return on the deceased's behalf if he or she received taxable income in the year of death.

Beware: As a survivor, this is a particularly emotional, difficult, and susceptible period in your life. Don't make any investments or loans; don't buy or sell any securities, annuities, or property; and don't convert any insurance policies *during this time.* Wait until you are in a more objective frame of mind and until you've had time to do research or consult with advisers.

Death and Taxes

Filing Your Income Tax Return

If you're a widow, you may be able to take advantage of a provision that gives you the benefit of joint-return rates for two years after your husband's death. In fact, you'll do much better on your taxes if you figure your tax as a joint filer instead of as a single person or even as a head of household.

In order to qualify, you must answer yes to the following questions:

- In the year your husband died, were you entitled to file jointly with him? (Whether you actually filed that way or not doesn't matter.)
- During this taxable year, was your home the principal residence of your children? You are disqualified if your children moved out permanently before the year ended or if in some other way they fail to qualify as your dependent(s).
- Have you provided over half the cost of maintaining your home?
    You also have to answer no to this one:
- Did you remarry?

As a surviving spouse, you can use this provision for the next two years. In other words, use the joint-return rates for 1985 and 1986.

If for some reason you fail to qualify, however, you might still be able to compute your tax using the head-of-household rates. As long as you remain single and your children live with you, you might qualify even if you can't claim exemptions for them. Discuss this matter with your accountant.

In Whose Name Should You Own Assets?

Taxes on securities sold after a spouse dies can differ considerably, depending on which form of ownership a husband and wife choose. There are several forms of ownership that a husband and wife can employ for their securities and other property.

Principally, these are outright single-party ownership ("fee simple") by either the husband or wife alone, or some form of joint ownership.

The two primary forms of joint ownership are joint tenancy and tenancy in common.

- *Joint tenancy* probably is the most common form of joint ownership. The distinctive characteristic of joint tenancy is the right of survivorship. Thus, on the death of one joint tenant, the survivor becomes the outright owner of the entire property without going through the costly, complex, and sometimes lengthy procedures of probate or court administration. A joint tenant cannot direct, by will or otherwise, that his or her interest go to anyone but the surviving joint tenant.

- *Tenancy in common:* Each tenant owns a partial interest in the entire property. Their interests usually, but not necessarily, are equal. On the death of one, the surviving tenant does not necessarily own the entire property. Instead, each deceased tenant's interest is distributed under the terms of his or her will; or if he or she dies without a will, according to the laws of intestacy of the state where the deceased resided. The interest of a tenant in common may, at his or her death, pass to the surviving spouse or children, or anyone else who may have been designated in the decedent's will.

During the lifetime of a husband and wife, it makes little difference whether securities and other property are owned entirely by one spouse or the other or owned jointly by both. But watch what happens when there is a death in the family:

Consider as an illustration two families who were wise enough to invest in the stock of IBM years ago.

The Morrisons and the Harrises each paid $5,000 for their shares of IBM stock. Each investment is worth $300,000 today.

The Morrisons' stock was registered in Mr. Morrison's name alone. The Harrises took title as joint tenants.

Both Mr. Morrison and Mr. Harris passed away recently. Sales of the IBM holdings are being discussed.

Mrs. Harris will have to concern herself with capital gains tax on such a sale. The Morrison family will not have this problem. Here's why:

In husband and wife joint ownership only one-half the value of the property is included in the estate of the spouse who dies first. But where property is owned outright, the full value is included in the estate.

However, property passing through an estate gets a "stepped-up" basis. Thus, to figure gain or loss, the cost basis of the property is its value for estate tax purposes; generally, the fair market value on the date of death.

Since all of Mr. Morrison's stock was included in his estate, its basis is stepped up to $300,000. A sale at about that amount yields little or no gain on which to pay tax.

Of course, if Mrs. Morrison had died before her husband, he would have continued his sole ownership with a basis of only $5,000. A sale by him then would produce an enormous capital gain.

As to the Harrises, only one-half of the stock is included in his estate and gets a stepped-up basis of $150,000. Mrs. Harris's one-half keeps the original basis of $2,500. Therefore, with a combined basis of $152,500, a sale for about $300,000 will produce a significant capital gain.

Unfortunately, there are no simple answers to the question of how to own property. Moreover, in some situations the form of ownership may be dictated by a third party. For example, in buying a home, many mortgage lenders require title to be taken in the names of both the husband and wife.

With a home there also is the enduring symbol of shared monetary and emotional interests in the property in the name of both spouses.

It's always advisable to obtain sound advice from an attorney or an accountant before committing substantial assets to a particular form of ownership, be it securities, home, or other property.

 BUDGET
MAKEOVERS

 ollowing are budget makeovers undertaken by *Sylvia Porter's Personal Finance Magazine* (SPPFM). We had experts take a look at the financial situation of different couples. In these examples you will see how love and money can work together—and perhaps you will see yourself as well.

MEET THE MOORES

The contents of Jim and Carole Moore's front hall closet in their new home held intriguing clues as to why the young California couple was seeking financial guidance: On the top shelf, in a two-foot pile, were board games, which included Rich Uncle, Payday, Black Jack, Risk, and the ever-popular Monopoly.

Like so many other young American couples, Jim, thirty-one, and Carole, twenty-nine, are concerned about money. At the depth of the '82 recession they had reached out boldly for a piece of the American dream: They bought their own home, complete with an acre of land and a frog-filled pond in Nipomo, in central California. However, in the space of only eleven months, not only had they moved into the $100,000 ranch house (with a mortgage payment, at 15½%, of $978 per month), they had produced their first child—a daughter, Kristen, born in September of 1982—and Jim had switched from full-time student to full-time industrial engineer on the Space Shuttle project at Vandenberg Air Force Base. That had meant a lot of changes in one year, they both agree now, looking back at the major transitions they'd accomplished in such a short time. And a lot of financial stress.

"When Jim was still in school and I was supporting us with my job as a career information specialist," Carole says, "we paid $190 a month in rent and barely squeaked by. Now we're living in a $100,000 house and together we make about $45,000 a year. But with the mortgage so high and everything else costing so much, the pressure still feels the same." Glancing around the sunny, well-equipped contemporary kitchen with its jaunty blue and white curtains she'd made herself, Carole laughed. "It's exactly the same strain as before—we've just upped our lifestyle!"

A good deal of the strain came from watching their money flow out each month at an alarming rate ever since they'd bought their house.

"Even though we're making $45,000 between us, which sounds like a lot, we've gotten accustomed to spending what we make," admitted Jim, a ruggedly handsome man who enjoys building furniture and doing his own home and car repairs. "Since buying the house, we've spent *more* than what we make. Even with my recent raise, we're still in the hole."

"We're falling behind quickly," Carole agreed worriedly. "We're always saying to each other we should go on a spending moratorium. We need help!"

The Moores are not fiscal incompetents—far from it. In fact, they had led their financial lives like many Americans caught in the vise of the high cost of living that has gripped thousands of young couples in the process of trying to establish their families and create an attractive lifestyle in which to bring up their children. And like so many two-income marriages, the pace of the Moores' lives and the quick series of major changes had prevented them from gaining an *overview* of how these life events had affected them financially.

It was this sense of fragmentation and anxiety that prompted the Moores to agree to let *Sylvia Porter's Personal Finance Magazine* assess their situation to see if there weren't a way to reallocate existing funds more sensibly and begin to plan their long-term financial future.

The day Libbie Agran, a well-known money manager from Los Angeles, walked into the Moores' lives, the couple began, for the first time in their six-year marriage, to get a clearer notion of how little they actually knew about themselves financially—and how simple it would be to gain that knowledge in order to start putting their financial house in order.

With a certain degree of embarrassment, Carole admitted, "Jim and I have one checking account and *two* checkbooks going constantly. Nobody keeps very good track, so we never know where we are. Sometimes we've been $600 off, and it's *never* in our favor."

Carole's confession sounded familiar. What people in a financial quandary need to do first, Agran explained to the Moores, is *get the facts.* "That means taking stock of your assets and liabilities."

Within a few hours, the Moores had pulled out boxes of paid bills, employment insurance policies, the odd file or two, scraps of paper—even jottings on the backs of envelopes—to find out what they owned . . . and what they owed. Between their checking account, an IRS refund due soon, and a money market account with $500 in it, they had $3,629 in cash, plus $1,744 in pension and profit sharing plans at Martin Marietta, the corporation Jim has worked for since graduating from engineering school. Much to their surprise, when they actually surveyed their possessions one by one (their cars, home furnishings, clothing, cameras, stereo, tools, kitchenware, silver, china—and even their records and tapes), they discovered they had more than $45,000 in personal possessions which they'd accumulated in more than six years of marriage. Their $100,000 house had appreciated $13,000, and their total assets came to a hefty $163,916.

"Now for the bad news," Carole groaned as she pulled out records of their charge accounts, bank cards, unpaid bills, and home mortgage papers. The Moores' total liabilities, including their $74,900 home mortgage, came to $75,600, leaving them a net worth of $88,316.

"Wow," Carole breathed, looking quite a bit more cheerful than she had when they'd been totaling up their debts.

"People are always surprised to find out they're worth more than they think they are," Agran said. "What's working against you at the moment, though, is your lack of financial planning beyond the short-term, and your lack of awareness of *where* that $45,000 a year is trickling out."

Agran has developed a sort of financial "passages" theory about people and their money. "Young couples like the Moores don't realize how much life will change for them over time," she says. "What goes on *now*, financially speaking, will be much different than what goes on five years from now."

Young adults have certain financial tasks to accomplish, which include some of the events the Moores have experienced: getting established in a career, attaining financial independence from parents, establishing a household and savings and checking accounts, getting credit, buying a car and furniture, and so on. The most common financial *errors* during the Young Adult Stage are overspending, failure to establish a pattern of good record-keeping, and failure to set financial goals. If these tasks aren't completed, Agran explained to the Moores, it's impossible, as the young couple had already discovered, to acquire an overall notion of a family's particular financial situation, and, more importantly, to keep rein on the outflow of money so a husband and wife can build for the future.

"What I'm seeing more and more in my practice," Agran told them, "is that two people in their thirties—both working—with what looks like lots of money coming in, still find they have debt piling up." One problem, she explained, is that with such healthy incomes, couples feel they should be able to vacation where they want, go out to dinner whenever they want, and do all the things their middle-class parents may have done. "But it's different now," she sympathized. "It takes a lot of planning just to stay even."

Refinancing a Must

For the Moores, the planning began by doing some research into the possibility of refinancing their expensive home mortgage, which they'd secured at a time of highest interest rates. When they'd bought the house in the spring of 1982, they hadn't checked around at various banks and savings and loans to compare interest rates, but had, instead, accepted the recommendation of their real estate agent, who'd steered them to an independent mortgage broker. The costs there were probably higher than what the Moores could have obtained at more traditional institutions. Meanwhile, mortgage rates had dropped somewhat, and Agran advised them to see if they couldn't get a better deal on a slightly larger loan of $80,000, putting the extra toward some house projects they had in mind.

Using a "financial diary" system of taking notes, Carole immediately called several local lenders, carefully noting the day, time of the call, the loan officer's name, and all pertinent information regarding the cost of borrowing money at each institution she talked to. The sheets of lined paper went into a three-ringed binder, along with the estimates of their assets, liabilities, and net worth. "You *must* commit the facts to paper," Agran emphasized. "One of the main problems you both have is that there are really no records."

"We promise to reform," Carole replied.

Setting Goals: From Jacuzzis to Retirement

Goal-setting can be another means by which people in financial confusion can straighten out their affairs. Young couples, Agran told them gently, tend to live only in the present. She reminded them of the series of life-stages she'd described earlier. "You need to begin to see much farther ahead than you do now."

Under *Short-term Goals* (1–12 months), the Moores listed landscaping their front yard (estimated to cost around $1,500, since Jim and Carole would do all the labor themselves); building their savings up $1,200 by saving $100 a month (hopefully through what they'd save if they refinanced the mortgage); building shelves throughout the house (the cost would be for materials only; Jim would do the work); a short vacation in Tahoe (minimal cost to be paid out of their income); analyzing their spending habits more thoroughly, and organizing their financial records (no cost; much time).

Without stopping to figure out yet how they would pay for them, their *Intermediate Goals* (1–5 years) broke down this way: birth of a second child; purchase of a new/used car or truck; nursery school for Kristen; child care for the new baby; landscaping the backyard, and building a deck and Jacuzzi adjacent to their master bedroom.

Looking at their long list, Jim added wistfully, "I'd sure like us to set up Individual Retirement Accounts." Nodding, they added IRAs to the list.

Neither Jim nor Carole had trouble identifying their *Long-term Goals:* a comfortable retirement; college educations for their youngsters. Carole anticipated they might move to a larger home; Jim wondered if he wouldn't enjoy someday managing real estate investments, since he was able to build and repair things and enjoyed the work immensely.

"Achievable goals," Agran said, "but you have to have a plan of action. It's not enough merely to *want* something and set a timetable. You've got to figure out *how* you're going to get there!"

The Moores and Agran brainstormed as to how the couple

could eventually get the money to fulfill the financial goals they had set. In addition to refinancing their home loan to reduce monthly payments and allow them to save at least $100 per month, the arithmetic showed that at the lower interest rate they could afford to tack on $5,100 to their existing $74,900 loan and still come out ahead. This could provide enough extra cash to landscape the front yard, and perhaps even remodel a breezeway to create a playroom or a room for a "mother's helper" student with whom they might exchange room and board for baby-sitting services, thus reducing child-care costs in the long run. Carole and Jim were more than willing to minimize costs by doing both home improvement projects themselves. "Don't neglect to put the same energy into the $100-a-month savings plan so you can build up your emergency cash to $5,000," Agran cautioned. "It's vital to have two- to three-month's salary as a cushion in case one of you becomes unemployed. You'll feel a lot less anxious about things."

Where Does All the Money Go?

Agran's next recommendation was that Jim and Carole spend a day or two reconstructing every penny they had spent in the previous three months. "I know it's an awful chore," she said, "but to make a break with your previous way of doing things, you've got to really *see* what's been happening to your money."

She pulled out a ledger that showed an example of simple, good recordkeeping. Every check each month was noted in one column and then listed a second time in its proper category, such as "home maintenance," "clothes," "entertainment," and so forth.

"You can use this easy system to keep track of what you're spending," Agran told them, pointing out the different columns, which were totaled at the bottom. "Immediately you'll see if you're spending too much on dinners out, or on items for the kitchen you can do without. With both of you filling in what you spend *as you spend it*, and discussing your financial picture at a set time once each month, you'll begin to set patterns for keeping things in order." What Agran found so beneficial about a system like this one is that "couples stop blaming each other for the mess things get into when husbands and wives have no real method for keeping track of things.

"I guarantee, once you see where the money is going, you will start re-ordering priorities to get to your goals."

Safekeeping

Agran also suggested the Moores rent a safe-deposit box to store important documents, such as their house deed, stock certificates or bonds, and documents of important life events, such as their marriage certificate, Kristen's birth records, Jim's military discharge records, and the like.

"Also, since you're being so virtuous," Agran laughed, "take that camera, Jim, and photograph a complete inventory of your household contents—including what's in the garage and your closets—for insurance purposes, and don't forget to take pictures of architectural detail." Agran explained that it's difficult to demand that an insurance company replace designer kitchen tile if a homeowner has no record of it. "If you don't have visual proof and your house burns down, you may end up with cheap Formica when the insurance company pays to rebuild your kitchen. And store those pictures in your safe-deposit box—not at home!"

Looking through the Moores' attractively decorated master bedroom to a big plate glass window framing the pond, Agran said suddenly, "Be sure you have at least $500,000 liability insurance in case someone falls into your pond. It's a fairly inexpensive add-on and it's worth it."

Agran's final recommendation for recordkeeping was to create a system of files: everything from paid bill stubs to income tax returns.

Looking Into the Future

Earlier in their discussion about the Moores' finances, Libbie Agran had been disturbed to discover the young couple had no will. "Part of the cost of having a baby is providing for that child if you die," she said. "I know that sounds grim, but it's a fact."

The Moores agreed they would make drawing up a will one of their first priorities. "It's been on our minds since she was born," Jim said sheepishly. "I guess it's one of those things you tend to put off."

The issue of wills brought up a discussion of life and disability insurance. "I get some life insurance automatically at work," said Jim.

Agran shook her head calmly. "That's good. It's my opinion that at your age, the purpose of insurance is to make it possible to take care of children, not adults. It covers the 'what ifs' and guarantees Kristen an education if something happens to either of you." Agran's recommendations were that Jim carry around $150,000 and Carole at least $70,000. "If one of you died and left $100,000, which the survivor invested at—say—12 percent, the income would net out at around $10,000 a year. That's not a fortune or a replacement for the lost salary, but it's helpful," she said.

Jim looked thoughtful. "I'll check at work to see what it would cost to up what I have." Carole agreed to do the same—both for life insurance and disability coverage.

"People often forget about disability," Agran noted. "But think about it. If one working parent isn't available because of illness or injury to care at all for a child and the other parent must continue to work full time to keep everything going, the loss of the other salary plus the cost of child care would be difficult and expensive without disability insurance."

The Cost of Children

When the Moores first began reviewing their finances, they had talked of having another baby early in 1985. After the discussion of insurance, Carole quietly calculated her current cost of child care for Kristen, since she planned to resume working full time at California Polytechnical College, a half hour from their home, once the second child had settled in. "By the time another baby was born," she said, adding up the numbers on her pad, "Kristen would be starting nursery school at about $2,000 a year, plus child care for the new baby would run about $2,400 a year." She stared at the figures. "With $40 a month for disposable diapers and $25 a month for formula—it'd cost us about $5,000 a year for two kids!"

"It's always a shock for parents to realize that with two children, you'll have a series of problems you don't have with one—and those problems cost money," empathized Agran. "You might want to find out from friends what an additional child meant to them financially. That kind of information can help you *time* your next child so it won't put undue strain on you or your budget, and you're bound to enjoy the experience a whole lot more—which is good for the new baby."

The Moores had said retirement plans and college education for their children were high priorities in terms of long-term goals. But the problem remained: how to get started on those far-off ideals when cash was so tight right now?

How to Begin Saving

Agran's recommendation was that as the Moores' spending on the little things slowed down, the couple would increase their contributions to the savings plan at Jim's company, which matches funds on an annual basis. "Also, Jim," Agran commented, "one way for someone as handy and healthy as you are to start accumulating money is to save with another goal in mind: in five to ten years you two can hope to buy a small fixer-upper duplex. You can earn income from it and eventually sell it at a profit. Perhaps later you could do the same thing with a small commercial building. This plan could be a nightmare for someone who couldn't do his own home repairs, but for you, it's a sound investment idea."

College education funds build up slowly, Agran continued. "Besides a regular savings plan, tell your relatives you're setting up an education fund for Kristen: all donations, large or small, are welcome!"

By the end of the long day's session, the Moores looked exhausted, but said they were tremendously relieved.

"This is exciting," Carole said, scrutinizing the list of items she and Jim were to research and decide on.

Libbie Agran filed her sheaves of notes into a trim briefcase. "I'd say you're in better shape than many couples your age. You've got your home; you've started your family; you've acquired a goodly amount of possessions; and you've both got useful talents in and outside your workplace. My parting recommendations are to cut down your spending on small things and change your emphasis to saving for the big things. You're in a hole right now, but not a deep hole. Your IRS refund will bail you out this time, but the biggest part of the equation is refinancing your home loan, becoming *systematic* about recordkeeping, and discussing money together. These are the devices that will get your finances under control."

In emphatic agreement with Agran about the need for an emergency reserve fund, Jay Rabinowitz, vice-president and manager of Merrill Lynch's Financial Planning Department, suggests a money market account or fund for that purpose. Funds can be opened at any brokerage firm and accounts at almost all banks. "The Moores should be sure that the bank type of account has no time limitations. Paying a penalty or being unable to withdraw the money defeats the purpose of the reserve.

"Once that $5,000 reserve has been established, the Moores should look toward growth-oriented investments because, hopefully, they will not be in need of the dividend income that more established stocks pay. I would recommend they begin their investing through a mutual fund, which would give them the advantage of wide diversification and professional management even though their investment may be modest."

Follow-Up

The Moores have followed through on most of the recommendations suggested by Libbie Agran. They refinanced their home mortgage, securing a variable rate mortgage at 10¾%, which has saved them $216 per month.

They have increased their liability insurance to $1 million, at an added cost of $76 per year. Both Carole and Jim were able to purchase additional amounts of life insurance at reasonable rates through their employee benefits plans at work, and added long-term disability protection.

They have paid off all credit card debt and cut down on nonessential purchases for themselves and the house. They have been able to save substantially more than the $100 per month Agran had recommended as a minimum, from money Jim made working overtime six weekends and by foregoing their trip to Lake Tahoe. Instead, they've been spending their free time gardening and landscaping. Kristen's "college fund" has been established at the bank and already contains contributions from her grandparents. The Moores have decided to delay having their second child by at least a year.

But like most people, Carole and Jim found some of their old habits hard to break.

"We have not reformed the way we write checks," Carole admitted sheepishly. "We each keep a checkbook going, and we haven't been totaling things up every week, the way Libbie said we should, but we're not overdrawn anymore, and we feel much more in control of our finances."

And what about making a will?

"We spoke to my brother the attorney about it," Carole said, embarrassed. "We . . . uh . . . promise to do it real soon."

"And we've filled out the application for a safe deposit box," Jim added quickly. "It's only $12 a year. We'll do that this week."

MEET THE SELFS

Roy and Marilyn Self are unusual among American couples. They have no perceptible financial problems.

They have a family income of $54,000 and, all things being equal, it has no place to go but steadily up. Roy represents Bowater Computer Forms in the Fort Worth-mid-cities area. The company is solid; the industry one of high growth. Marilyn works about twenty hours a week with American Airlines as a sales agent in the tour and international department—a position that qualifies her and her family for enviable travel privileges.

They are a stunning couple in their forties with three healthy, energetic, and intelligent daughters: Andrea, sixteen; Gena, thirteen; and Ashley, nine.

Their charming Spanish-style home is surrounded by lush Texas foliage. You don't realize it, of course, but the mortgage on that warmly appointed $115,000 home is a mere $25,000. And they have very little else in the way of debt.

So why now—when pennies are no more to them than fillers for a brandy snifter—are they experiencing a vague sense of uneasiness about their financial situation?

What propelled Roy to the E. F. Hutton office of Jeanette Alexander on April 14, 1983, to ask about financial planning services? Two things.

Roy and Marilyn were aware that 1982 was the last time income-averaging would benefit the family's tax bill unless one of them had an unexpected jump in income.

They were straddling two age groups. They were young enough to feel well, keep physically active, and see growth in their earning power. And they were at the age where it was time to think about the immediate goal of sending the kids to college, to contemplate retirement, and to concern themselves with the possibility of illness or disability.

"You can and should be proud of yourselves," Von Smith, a certified financial planner (CFP) from Fort Worth told Marilyn and Roy after he had spent several days studying their financial position and reviewing their stated goals.

"Intuitively you've taken a conservative approach to your financial planning," Smith said. "Your lifestyle matches your ability to pay for it. That's a comfortable spot to be in when we talk about the future. Relax. You're going to reach all the goals you've set for yourselves."

Here is what their overall financial position looked like as of July 1983.

ROY & MARILYN SELF FINANCIAL STATEMENT 7/23/83

ASSETS		LIABILITIES		NET VALUE
Cash & Checking		Credit Cards & Department Store Account Balances		
Checking	$ 2,000	Total Due	$ 2,000	$ 0
Savings	2,950			2,950
Credit Union	1,000			1,000
Subtotal	$ 5,950		$ 2,000	$ 3,950
Investments				$ 600
12 sh AT&T	$ 600			
Mutual Funds				1,610
Growth Fund	1,610			1,060
Emerging Growth	1,060			
IRA—Growth	2,210	Deferred Income	$ 1,000	1,210
		Tax + 10%	$ 1,000	$ 4,480
Subtotal	$ 5,480			
Personal Assets				
Home	$115,000	Mortgage	$25,000	$ 90,000
Van	17,000	Credit Union for Van	10,000	7,000
Household Goods	17,000	Furniture Store	200	16,800
Land	5,000			5,000
Subtotal	$154,000		35,200	$118,800
Combined Totals	$165,430		$38,200	$127,230

Goal I: Provide 60 Percent of Daughters' College Expenses

"I don't think you should force kids to go to college," Roy said. "Personally, I didn't find the experience particularly worthwhile. I think I would have profited more from learning a trade.

"But if my kids are really motivated, I'd like to help them. With the cost of education being so great, they really do need the financial help."

Marilyn, who graduated valedictorian of her high school but who never went on to college, puts more stock in a four-year education. Getting a degree is still on her mind; she feels having it would improve her self-confidence. She has taken some courses at Southern Methodist University but doesn't plan to matriculate—at least not now. She feels this is the time to concentrate on the children's education. "Nonetheless," she says, "I'm not sure I'd want to go into debt to finance it. I'd rather work longer hours."

Smith suggested that neither might be necessary. Paying for college through interest-free loans to the children might be the answer. "If you could accumulate enough cash to make loans to your daughters," he said, "they could receive the interest or dividends in a much lower tax bracket. If properly arranged, you can lend the money to the girls and not charge them any interest. The loan would be repayable on demand when the need for college money has ended."

Huddled around the kitchen table, the three pored over the figures. Smith's plan was based on borrowing money—about $90,000—this year.

"If you go to the bank and explain what you're doing—borrowing money to invest in CDs fo you children's education, you should be able to negotiate a spread—the difference between the interest you pay on the loan and the interest you get on the CDs—of between 1 and 2 percent.

"It's a good deal for the bank," Smith explained. "The money never leaves the premises; there's little risk that the girls are going to come marching in and withdraw the money from their CDs; and the bank is building goodwill with a customer."

Such a loan, Smith explained, would cost the Selfs—over a fifteen-year period—about $57,000 in after-tax dollars. The amount netted by the children would be approximately $78,500. (All amounts are stated in 1983 dollars.)

Without this income shifting, the Selfs would have to earn approximately $136,000 for their children to have $78,000 for college.

Goal 2: Keeping Taxes As Low As Possible

Because the spiritual side of their lives is very important to them, Marilyn and Roy make sizable contributions to their church.

"No less charitable, however," Smith explains, "would be to donate an asset—of equal worth to the cash you now give—that has grown substantially in value from when you purchased it.

"The church can sell the asset—say, your appreciated shares in your growth fund—for cash or use it for church activities without paying income taxes on the increase in value. You, on the other hand, can deduct the full value of the asset and not have to report the increased value as income, as you would have to do if you had sold the asset and donated the cash."

Smith's second tax recommendation was to use two IRAs, one for Marilyn and one for Roy (instead of just one for Roy) to create a $4,000 deduction, rather than the $2,000 they had taken last year.

And finally, counseled Smith, "You have reached the magic income level for increased chances of IRS audit of your returns. A certified public accountant might be a good adviser for you at this point. Not only will a CPA be likely to figure your taxes accurately, but also you will have an experienced tax expert to deal with the IRS if they challenge any of your deductions."

Goal 3: Retirement Without Concern

"If we can't save much each year because of all our present financial responsibilities, how can we possibly expect our current lifestyle to continue when we retire twenty years from now?" Marilyn's question seemed as if it echoed in millions of homes across the country.

To her surprise and to Roy's, Smith showed them how, without even realizing it, they were saving impressive sums toward retirement. From their annual savings—the two IRAs, their two companies' pension plans, the Bowater savings plan to which Roy

RETIREMENT SAVINGS AND INCOME

SOURCE	ANNUAL ADDITION	20- YEAR TOTAL	INCOME /YR.	LESS TAXES	NET INCOME
Roy's IRA	$ 2,000	$ 40,000	$ 2,000	$ 215	$ 1,785
Marilyn's IRA	2,000	40,000	2,000	215	1,785
Marilyn's Pension	co.'s contrib.	co's contrib.	5,000	540	4,460
Roy's Pension	co's contrib.	co's contrib.	14,200	1,530	12,670
Bowater Savings	2,700	54,000	2,700	290	2,410
Social Security	6,800	136,000	12,000	?	12,000
TOTALS	$13,500	$270,000	$37,900	$2,790	$35,110

ASSUMPTIONS:
1. All amounts expressed in 1983 dollars. Investment return equals inflation rate. Therefore $1,000 saved will produce $1,000 of buying power when withdrawn.
2. Amounts accumulated are withdrawn over 20 years at the same rate of buying power, except Social Security, which is not related to contributions directly.
3. Annual additions include employer contributions if known.
4. Company contributions fluctuate but income estimates per year after 20 years come from projections on both companies' benefits statements.
5. Pension benefits are based on current income levels and assume continuous employment to age 65.
6. Income taxes are prorated over taxable income. Taxation of Social Security benefits will remain unchanged.

subscribes, and Social Security—they discovered they needn't do any more than what they are doing already to assure themselves of a retirement income commensurate with what they have now.

Goal 4: Enough Insurance

Concern over enough insurance was prompted by the question: What if one of us becomes disabled or dies?

The Selfs want to be certain that there would be enough income for the other spouse and the children to continue living in their current lifestyle.

Although it appeared that the Selfs have adequate life and disability insurance, Smith suggested they meet with their agent and reassess the picture. He suggested that the cash value of Roy's life policies be borrowed to the maximum each year to help the Selfs make the interest-free loans to the children or to invest that money to receive a higher rate of return, or to reduce annual premiums.

"Also, you might think about electing the 'Interest Only' settlement option on all of your life insurance policies. This election assures you that the money will be earning interest from the moment the insured dies until the survivors are able to think straight enough to decide what to do with the proceeds."

"I Must Get Organized"

Marilyn, the keeper of the checkbook, preparer of tax returns, and person generally in charge of monitoring the family finances, has a feeling she's losing control over the whole operation.

She's writing more checks than ever—an average of 67 a month—to avoid being drawn into a possible overuse of their credit cards that would have them paying the 18 percent annual interest bank cards are charging on unpaid balances. But she's not happy about the extra time this check-writing is taking.

Roy takes blank checks from the back of their joint checkbook and forgets to enter the amount he spends. The frequent overdraft notices (as a result of Marilyn thinking they have more money in their account than they actually do) are not only embarrassing; they're also costly.

To eliminate the massive daily check-writing Marilyn is slave to, Smith suggested she open charge accounts at specific stores where she does regular business—the grocery, the cleaners, drugstore, and the like. There is less temptation to overspend at an individual store (especially one without any particular glamour attached to it) than there is with a general all-purpose bank credit card. "It will consolidate payments and save check-writing time," Smith promised. "And look for special promotions on credit cards for which you pay no interest if you pay within thirty days."

Smith suggested Roy open a separate checking account for his occasional and personal use. Marilyn would write him a monthly check from their joint account to be used for this personal account. That way, any forgotten entries would not bring surprise shortages in the joint account.

Organization of bills, records, and other financial information is always a headache, Smith assured the Selfs, "but less painful if you're organized." He pulled file boxes, manila envelopes, and other forms out of his briefcase. It was just a preview, for Smith was to meet with Marilyn again to go over the specifics of keeping track of income and expenses—all of which would help her when she prepared 1983's tax return.

Living Now

Because Roy and Marilyn are trying to develop a balanced lifestyle—neither thinking only of today nor squirreling away every extra cent—Smith's suggestion to travel more evoked a "that's just what we wanted to hear" reaction from them.

"I realize this idea goes against the traditional wisdom of saving every nickel for college and retirement," Smith said, "but take advantage of Marilyn's marvelous travel benefits. You have the time and the money to travel with the children now. In a few years either they won't want to travel with you or they will be off in different directions. If for some reason your daughters went to work for a year or two before going to college, the experience and maturity gained through travel would help them enormously—both in the work force and in their higher education."

Marilyn and Roy nodded in agreement. They obviously want to turn their dream of visiting Europe into reality.

Although the services rendered by the Personal Financial Management Department of E. F. Hutton normally cover all areas of personal finance, we asked them to limit their comments on the Selfs' budget makeover to the investment area for the children's education funds. Sylvia J. Pozarnsky, vice-president, responded.

"Before relying on any technique to deflect income to the children, as through the use of interest-free loans, the Selfs should evaluate with an attorney the chances that such an arrangement would be upheld in their own jurisdiction if challenged by the Internal Revenue Service. Should they wish to proceed with interest-free loans, we would concur with the use of CDs for at least a portion of the funds invested for the children, despite the potential disadvantages that: 1) there is a penalty for early withdrawal of funds; and 2) the interest rate normally is fixed, thus preventing investors from taking advantage of higher rates, if available, during the term of the CD. (That fixed rate is beneficial of course, if interest rates decline.)

"The Selfs should be careful to structure the maturity dates of the CDs to correspond with the date or dates that funds will be needed (e.g., Andrea is already sixteen and may need educational assistance in just two years), to avoid paying a premature-withdrawal penalty.

"To assure liquidity, they should also consider using a money market fund or account for at least a portion of the funds."

Follow-Up

After the Selfs met with Von Smith in July and August of '83, they became immersed in family matters. Marilyn's father died. Roy's mother, who had been fighting cancer for a year, needed nursing home care. Marilyn, who never appreciated her flexible schedule at American Airlines more, has spent most of her time shuttling between mothers—caring for, comforting, and looking after the affairs of both hers and Roy's.

"Because of this we didn't move as rapidly as we would have liked to on our financial plans," Marilyn explained three months later. "We especially want to find out more about the interest-free loans to the children for their education—and within the next month we hope to meet with our bank to discuss it. But as of now, all we've done is get our bookkeeping in order. We are becoming aware of our finances because we've been logging our expenses and income. The big surprise to me was how much we spend at the grocery store—approximately $300 a month. I think that's a lot, because we eat out frequently."

As part of their new awareness, the Selfs bought a cassette course on time management. "Though Von suggested the children might benefit from it as much as we might," Marilyn said, "they are unenthusiastic about listening and not particularly happy with the idea of structure that time management suggests. If we can't get them to listen to the tapes during dinner, I don't think we have a chance of getting them to sit down during the evening. They're just too busy."

As for traveling, Roy and Marilyn are talking about going to London. They have until April to take advantage of a free standby American Airlines pass. As tempting as that sounds, their family responsibilities are so heavy that a vacation abroad will have to remain a last-minute decision.

MEET THE JACKSONS

Don and Carmen Jackson's farmhouse, nestled cozily in the fertile countryside outside of Madison, Wisconsin, is a sight straight out of a Currier & Ives print. Nothing dispels that atmosphere when you enter this vibrant couple's home. Two merrily barking dogs welcome you into a sunny kitchen filled with the aroma of baking bread. Two exuberantly healthy, ruddy-cheeked children—Kyle, five, and Kimberly, two—complete the picture.

But Don, thirty-nine, and Carmen, thirty-eight, are a far cry from a typical country couple. Granted, they thrive on the simpler practices of centuries past, such as chopping wood and harvesting vegetables. But Don, a transplanted Brooklynite, and Carmen, originally from Lima, Peru, also thrive on their high-powered, high-pressured jobs. Don is a senior consultant at Development Alternatives, Inc., a firm that works with the federal government in the design and implementation of overseas agricultural programs. Carmen is the producer/director of ethnic programming at a major radio station in Madison. Together they made close to $45,000 last year.

So it's no surprise that the Jacksons, like so many American couples in mid-career, have their minds on a topic that is distinctly pragmatic and presentday: They want to know how they can improve the management of their financial life.

What exactly are the Jacksons' financial concerns?

Cash Flow

Don is in a classic Catch-22 situation. His job can net him close to $50,000 annually, an ample amount to cover bills and contribute to savings. But Don's field is international agricultural economics. If he were on the job all year, he would also be out of the country for most of it, leaving him with virtually no time to spend with Carmen, Kyle, and Kimberly. As a result, Don chooses to work on a project-to-project basis—and that means irregular paychecks.

Don and Carmen agree that cash flow is a perennial problem.

"I'll receive a large check after a few months of no checks," says Don, "and then, before we know what has happened, we've spent it all paying bills and buying things for the house."

Carmen's $10,000 salary—she works a 25-hour week—goes almost entirely to payments on the $30,000 in second mortgages they took out last year to fund the additions to their house.

"While it's not as bad as feast or famine, it gets a little too close for comfort," says Don. "Right now our money flow is sporadic; what we need is a steady stream."

Home Improvements

The Jacksons' property includes eighteen acres of land, six of which are leased to a local farmer for $360 a year.

They bought the house eight years ago for a modest $41,000; it is now valued at $200,000. Not only did Carmen and Don completely renovate the existing structure, they excavated an old cistern to make a combination cold storage/wine cellar, added a walk-in solar collector, and built two entirely new wings.

The problem is that the renovation is not yet completed. The polished pewter and custom upholstered furniture of one room leads to the newly spackled Sheetrock of the next.

"We'd really like to wrap up the renovation at this point," says Carmen, "so we can go on to other things."

How to finance the finishing touches, as well as find the time to make them, are top priority issues for the Jacksons.

Sideline Business

At one point, Don thought he might want to go into the furniture refinishing business full time. He invested close to $25,000 in a franchise agreement and the stripping equipment, and even gave the business a name: Roaring Rooster Restorations. His parents, who moved from New York to the nearby town of Lodi to be near their only son and his family, now own an antique shop. Don would have had both an instant customer and a referral service for his venture.

"But I had a trial period of sorts when I was home for a long stretch between projects," explains Don. "I found I became very bored and restless working with my hands full time. I didn't realize until then how much I prosper on the intellectual stimulation and challenge of my job.

"Now I could use some ideas on what to do with the business—all the equipment is just sitting there."

Providing for the children's education, getting more insurance, and starting a retirement fund were just a few of the other concerns that made the Jacksons so eager for financial planner Mary Merrill's advice. When Merrill arrived at the Jackson house in Poynette, on January 27, 1984, she came equipped with a thick stack of papers entitled "Goal-Oriented Financial Plan for Don and Carmen Jackson." She had developed it after a two-hour meeting with the Jacksons at her Madison office three weeks before. At that time, the Jacksons had filled out numerous personal and financial data forms and had also discussed many of their problems and priorities.

Almost immediately upon entering the Jacksons' house, Merrill noticed the antiques: "These are a big asset, but they're not reflected in the forms you filled out. Have you ever had them appraised?"

Don said they hadn't.

"I'm sure your parents—through their antique-shop acquaintances—could find someone to do it for you," said Merrill. "Put 'appraisal' at the top of your list of things to do. And photograph every item. That way you'll have some backup evidence if you ever are forced to make a fire or theft insurance claim."

Don and Carmen then sat down with Merrill, each with a copy of the printed financial plan, for what would turn out to be a four-hour brainstorming, discussion, and question/answer session.

"First let's take a look at how your assets measure up against your liabilities," Merrill began.

Based on the information the Jacksons had given her, Merrill calculated their assets. Their savings, company stock valued at $15,000, an IRA with $2,000 in it, the house at resale value of $200,000, and all their personal property added up to a hefty $283,640.

"Don't we have some bonds, too?" Carmen asked Don.

"That's right. They're somewhere upstairs in my office. Come to think of it, a lot of them have probably matured."

"Chcek with your banker about those bonds," Merrill said, "because, whether or not they have matured, this could be the right time to cash in at least some of them." She also suggested the Jacksons keep their bonds in a safe-deposit box and have a list on file showing the name of each bond, its amount, and its maturity date.

In the liability column, the Jacksons had only two items: $55,000 in mortgage and home improvement loans and approximately $2,000 in unpaid bills and credit card debts. Their total net worth came to $226,640.

"That's encouraging," said Don, "but it never feels like we have that much."

"Probably because most of your assets are not in the form of disposable funds," Merrill said. "You only have $750 in your savings account. The bulk of your worth rests in items like your house, cars, furniture—things you are not about to trade in for cash."

As the Jacksons and Merrill moved to the next page of the plan, titled "Clients Goals," Merrill explained her feelings on financial planning: "It is a process, not a product. It's not a static or ironclad thing." She believes that financial plans should be regularly updated to take into account all the various changes a client experiences in income, outlook, and aspirations.

"So," she continued, "never feel locked into a plan. You—and it—are bound to change with time.

"But now let's get to the nitty-gritty: your financial objectives and how to achieve them," said Merrill.

Objective 1: Stretch present cash flow and develop regular savings plan.

Merrill first suggested the Jacksons explore the possibility of refinancing the two second-mortgage loans they have with the University of Wisconsin Credit Union. They got their first mortgage from Don's parents, and its terms are unbeatable: $25,000 at 5 percent interest, payable over 20 years.

Don seemed surprised: "You think I could do better than I did with the credit union? When I took out the loans last year, they had the best terms available."

"Let's take a careful look at them," suggested Merrill.

Don brought an accordion folder from his office, located the agreements, and gave them to Merrill to examine.

"I doubt you could do much better than this one for $15,000 at 11.75 percent payable over 10 years," Merrill said. "But this second loan for $15,000 is at 14 percent and requires a balloon payment after two years. Mortgage rates have come down, at least temporarily. With some careful shopping around, you may be able to reduce the interest rate on this loan, increase the number of years, and decrease your monthly payment. Watch out for any bank charges in the form of points, though. They could wipe out the savings of refinancing."

Merrill explained that the secret to financial independence "is not brilliance or luck, but discipline—the discipline to save part of all your earnings and put it to work for you. An initial budget requires some time, effort, and sacrifice, but the economic and psychological benefits more than justify the effort."

"Where do we begin?" asked Carmen.

"Start by looking at last year's figures," Merrill advised. She then directed the Jacksons' attention to the income/expenditure sheet she had compiled, based on the 1983 data they had given her. Here's what it looked like:

FAMILY BUDGET ILLUSTRATION

INCOME	AMOUNT	EXPENDITURES	AMOUNT
Salary—husband	$33,500	Income taxes	7,443
Salary—wife . . .	9,600	Social Security (F.I.C.A.). . .	2,839
Interest.	100	Mortgage payments	5,740
Dividends	100	Property tax	860
Rentals.	360	Utilities.	1,500
Total income . .	43,660	Home maintenance	10,000
		Auto operation	2,150
		Auto insurance.	177

INCOME	AMOUNT	EXPENDITURES	AMOUNT
		Education/reading	500
		Clothing	2,000
		Food	5,200
		Life insurance	400
		Medical insurance	200
		Medical expense..........	200
		Property & casualty insurance	431
		Entertainment	300
		Child care...............	720
		Miscellaneous.............	1,450
		Total spending	$42,110
		Balance available for savings and investment..........	$ 1,550

"Now I know where it all goes!" exclaimed Don.

"Wow," added Carmen. "I never thought we spent so much on food over the course of a year."

Objective 2: Make a realistic month-by-month budget.
Merrill advised the Jacksons to make an annual budget based on these 1983 figures. "Just put your projected figures for 1984 next to last year's numbers. In 1983, for example, you spent $2,000 on clothes. If you think that is an area you can cut back on, enter $1,500 as the 1984 figure. That puts you $500 ahead already.

"Then break the budget down into months. In months when your income is larger than budgeted, put the excess into savings. That way you'll have it to draw on in the months when your income is less than average."

Merrill advised the Jacksons to structure their budget in the following manner:

1) Earmark a fixed total for savings and put that aside first. Allocate set sums for education and retirement accumulation.
2) Put other fixed expenses next. Include debt repayment obligations in this category.

3) Remaining funds are for discretionary expenses, including home renovation.
4) Keep records of income and expenditures.
5) Set strict spending limits.

Another suggestion from Merrill: "Build up your savings account to $1,000 and then transfer that money to a high-paying money market fund with check-writing privileges. Once you've satisfied the requirements for opening the account, most money market accounts will accept deposits of any size, however small."

"I never realized you could write checks on a money market account," said Don.

"Most accounts automatically issue you a checkbook," explained Merrill. "You can usually only write checks for $500 or more, but that works to your advantage: You don't draw off and deplete the account in little dribs and drabs that way—every withdrawal gets careful consideration when it's such a large amount."

Objective 3: Complete the restoration of the house.
"Right now," Merrill pointed out, "you have two very strong forces pulling at you. On the one hand, you want to begin saving systematically; but on the other, you'd like to get your house finished once and for all.

"I'll be frank," she continued. "You're both nearing forty, and while that's far from old, if you don't start saving now—for the children's education and for your retirement—you may run into serious trouble later.

"After savings, however, I don't see anything wrong with putting the rest into your house," added Merrill. "Your house and antiques will probably be the biggest investments you make in life. And while you may not get the same high return as someone who invests in stocks or rental real estate, you're getting a return in terms of pride, satisfaction, and enjoyment—things that are worth a lot but don't have a price tag."

"But do you think we'll really have any money left over after saving?" asked Don.

"By refinancing your mortgage, cashing in those matured bonds, and diverting money from other areas to pad the home-improvement budget, there's a good chance you'll find the funds you need," Merrill said.

Objective 4: Explore opportunities for recouping the $25,000 investment in the furniture-refinishing business.

"I don't really want to sell the business," said Don. "Once I've finished work on the house, it could be a good way to make extra income between projects. Right now, though, I don't have the time, money, or driving interest to really get it going."

Merrill's suggestion: Find someone, perhaps a retiree or someone in need of a second income, who would be interested in starting up the business. Offer him or her a percentage of the profits rather than a salary.

"Owning a sideline business could have tax advantages for you," Merrill advised. "Even if you break even to the penny by setting up the business, at least you can depreciate the cost of all that equipment on your income tax return."

Objective 5: Increase insurance funds.

The Jacksons, it turns out, have excellent property, liability, and major medical insurance, as well as adequate income-continuation protection from Don's employer.

"The area I suspect we're deficient in is life insurance," said Don. "I am covered for $64,000 and Carmen is covered for $33,000."

"At the bare minimum, Don should be insured for an additional $50,000," said Merrill, "to cover the repayment of the mortgage debt and loans."

The Jacksons pay approximately $400 a year for $20,000 of whole life insurance. Merrill suggested that for the same premium the Jacksons (as non-smokers) could get $200,000 of term insurance for the next five years. That would safeguard the immediate future, providing for such things as the children's education and Carmen's retirement at a price they could afford.

"How do I go about converting my policy?" asked Don.

"Simply establish a new policy and then cancel and cash in your old one—but make sure you do it in that order," Merrill counseled.

Objective 6: Accumulate funds for the children's education.

Merrill recommended that the Jacksons set up a mutual-fund account for each child, using the children's Social Security numbers. The Jacksons would then be exempt from paying taxes on interest from that money, under the Uniform Gifts to Minors Act. Instead, the children, who are in a much lower tax bracket, pay the tax (if any). Once the funds reach a certain level, Carmen and Don would be required to file income tax forms in the children's names.

Merrill calculated the funds required for the children's education, based on the assumptions that the annual expense in today's dollar would be $4,000, and the annual rate of inflation would be 5 percent.

If the Jacksons waited until Kyle and Kimberly were of college age and tried to pay their education expenses with taxable out-of-pocket income, they would need $73,651.

But if Don and Carmen put $74 a month into an account that gets a 10 percent return for Kyle and $49 a month in a similar account for Kimberly the tuition would be taken care of by the time they are ready for college.

"I realize," says Merrill, "that many colleges are more expensive than the $4,000-a-year mark we've set. But I think the $123 is a realistic amount for you to start saving every month and, at the very least, you'll have half their expenses set aside."

"If either of them plans to go to Harvard or Princeton," Don interjected, "I'm sure we'd be able to tap the various scholarship sources for help at that point."

Objective 7: Accumulate funds for retirement.

"I'd like to keep contributing to my IRA," says Don, "but other than that, I don't consider this a top priority."

Don's parents are moderately well off and he's an only child.

This provides him with a measure of financial security many people don't have.

But Merrill suggested that Don broach the subject of finances with his parents: "Most parents would like to have the opportunity to discuss their death plans with their children, but are afraid to upset them. I think you should try to talk to your parents and get an idea of what the financial picture really is."

Merrill also thought the Jacksons should try to put the maximum in their IRA each year: "Since your marginal combined federal and state tax bracket is 33 percent, or $1,320 of every $4,000, the actual cost of saving the maximum IRA amount of $4,000 for you is only $2,680."

Merrill then told Don and Carmen what so many couples have heard before (and so many neglect to do anything about): Wills are a must.

"What about do-it-yourself wills?" asked Don.

"I wouldn't risk it. They often don't hold up in court," answered Merrill. "Remember, a will doesn't have to be an expensive proposition. Ask your lawyer beforehand how much it will cost you. Then arrive at the office with a complete list of your stocks, bonds, insurance policies, mortgages, and personal possessions. It will save your lawyer time, which means it will save you money."

By the end of the session, both Don and Carmen looked a little overwhelmed, but they also seemed full of hope.

"Can you think of any other questions?" asked Merrill in wrapping up.

"No," replied Don and Carmen in unison. "Now we have to sit down and figure out what to do first!"

Follow-Up

Six weeks later, the Jacksons were in the process of following through on many of Merrill's recommendations. They had started drafting their wills, investigating new life insurance policies, and shopping for second mortgage loans with lower interest rates and

206 / LOVE AND MONEY

longer terms. In addition, they had earmarked $500 to make their first regular monthly deposit to a savings account.

"We've really only just begun to make headway," explained Don, "because right after our meeting with Mary, I was called to Washington for several weeks. I couldn't get started on a lot of things that I wanted to since I was busy with work and away from home.

"One change I've noticed already, though," he continued, "is that Carmen and I are doing a lot more long-term planning. We've really revised our way of thinking about our finances." For instance, both the Jacksons feel that renovating their house is now secondary to accumulating savings. "While we're not going to stop working on it, both of us are very serious about setting and sticking to our home-improvement spending limits."

Any other resolutions? Both Don and Carmen are eager to make further contributions to their IRAs. "And we really must get our antiques appraised," adds Don. "That's something I've been meaning to do for a long time."

MEET THE FAERMANS

Tio, a flamboyant, blue-and-gold parrot, alerted his owners, Shari and Gustavo Faerman, that visitors had arrived at the door of their house. The noisy bird continued to caw and cackle during the time it took Gustavo to pad through the living room and open the front door. The Faermans' home, a rented condo, is nestled in the hills of Westlake Village, a community outside of Los Angeles.

"We just got up," Gustavo grinned sheepishly at his guests. "We hardly ever get to sleep in. We've been working seven days a week, ten to twelve hours a day," he apologized, welcoming his visitors inside. "It's a real luxury having an appointment at home at ten o'clock in the morning."

Libbie Agran, the Los Angeles financial expert sent in by *SPPFM*, introduced herself and her companions, and explained that she was going to spend the day assessing the plight of the two young entrepreneurs.

The Faermans' first-year problems in launching their restaurant, *Pollo Supremo*, were typical of those experienced by many of the people who start their own businesses.

Gustavo, thirty, an Argentinian whose family had moved to the United States when he was thirteen, headed for the kitchen and began brewing coffee for his guests.

While he set out breakfast pastries and coffee cake on the kitchen table, he related a bit of his personal history. After graduating from an eastern junior college in 1976, Gustavo had worked for nearly a decade in the food business.

"I did everything from making salads at a ski resort, to catering weddings and bar mitzvahs, to spinning records at a discotheque," he said. "My most valuable experience was as assistant manager of a pancake restaurant in Beverly Hills."

Gustavo met his wife, Shari, twenty-nine, when they were teenagers, but the couple had gone their separate ways after high school.

After graduating from college, Shari had worked for a cosmetic business and in advertising and public relations for a weight-loss clinic. Gustavo and Shari, now both living in California, were reunited through family acquaintances and were married in 1981.

A year later, they borrowed $64,000, using Shari's father's home as collateral, to buy *Pollo Supremo*, an existing restaurant in the predominantly Hispanic community of Oxnard, sixty-five miles north of Los Angeles.

The Faermans acknowledged that they had probably paid too much for their business and had been drastically undercapitalized to begin with. Now, Gustavo said, although the couple had favorably renegotiated the balance owed on the original deal, they had already committed themselves to opening a second restaurant in a few weeks (one they were starting up themselves, unlike *Pollo Supremo*, which they had taken over). This despite the fact that their first venture had been showing a deficit of about

$2,000 per month. Shari's father had been contributing additional capital as needed, but the money squeeze was affecting every aspect of their lives.

When the Faermans had decided to open the second restaurant—in nearby Santa Paula—business loans totaling $147,000 were secured by a third-trust deed on Shari's parents' home (which was valued at $327,000, minus a longstanding $40,000 mortgage). Shari and Gustavo's share of the $211,000 debt came to $105,000. The official partnership for both restaurants consisted of Gustavo, the working partner (although Shari worked nearly full time, unsalaried, in management, marketing, and promotion), and his father-in-law, the financial partner.

Here's the sequence of events in the purchases of the businesses:

> Purchase of first restaurant (January 1983)
> PRICE: $140,000
> FINANCING: Down payment of $50,000 with owner-carried financing of $90,000 at 12 percent.
> SOURCE OF FUNDS: Gustavo's father-in-law borrowed $64,000 from a savings and loan, using his home as collateral. Monthly payments of $838.48 are made to the savings and loan from the business.
> JANUARY 1984: The balance of the loan was now $87,000 and the restaurant was losing money. A decision was made to open the second restaurant in Santa Paula. Gustavo and his father-in-law met with the former owner of the Oxnard restaurant and offered to pay him in cash if he would accept $65,000 as balance due, thus reducing the purchase price of the Oxnard restaurant from $140,000 to $115,000.

In January, Gustavo and his father-in-law arranged another loan for $147,000 from Topa Leasing using the father-in-law's home as collateral. The home is now fully encumbered:

Value of home	$327,000
1st trust deed	(40,000)
2nd trust deed	(64,000)
3rd trust deed	(147,000)
Equity	$ 78,000

The $147,000 loan was used as follows:

$ 65,000	to pay off former owner of the first restaurant
82,000	to open the second restaurant
$147,000	

The Topa loan is a variable-interest-rate loan starting at 15.56 percent and structured as a lease for 84 months, with payments of $3,170.29 per month. The first payment was due March 10, 1984.

As Gustavo poured the fresh-perked coffee, Shari appeared carrying Tio on her arm and installed him on his perch out on the porch.

"Our basic problem," she said, "is that we're not showing any profit at the restaurant because of all the money we owe."

In other words, the Faermans were severely undercapitalized.

"Cash flow has been our biggest problem," Shari continued. "We were not very well financed going into this venture and we can't seem to get ahead of the monthly payments to make any money."

"We're also dealing with the problem of unreliable help," Gustavo added, "and that's frustrating." He explained that during the previous four weeks, they had somehow managed to serve some 4,800 meals, despite the fact that four of their six staff members had failed to show up for work.

As financial expert Libbie Agran began looking over the papers the Faermans had presented for her inspection, Shari glanced around the kitchen table at her visitors and laughed nervously.

"Owning your own restaurant . . . it's everybody's dream—right?"

Or nightmare. According to the Small Business Administration, 50 percent of all small businesses go bankrupt within a year. Nine out of ten fail within three years. A study completed by Dun & Bradstreet in the mid-seventies attributed 91 percent of the failures to inefficient management.

Shari and Gustavo acknowledge that before entering into their entrepreneurial venture, they were impulsive and occasionally compulsive spenders—in other words, inefficient managers of their *own* finances.

"Buying things makes me feel good," Shari said almost apologetically. "I had a bad habit of spending compulsively and I've been working on it for two years. I still go out and buy things I know we can't afford, but now it's a lot more manageable."

Agran noted that the Faermans had let debt creep up on them, with nearly $450 owing in clothing expenses, $2,145 in home-furnishing bills, plus nearly $3,500 outstanding for other personal items, such as entertainment and car repair, on their MasterCard and Balance Plus bank accounts.

"When I was much younger, I used to spend, spend, spend," Gus agreed, "so in a way, I was very understanding of what Shari was going through."

Taking into account the debts they had brought into the marriage and such long-term debt as an education loan of $3,075 and an auto loan of $7,590, the Faermans were in the unhappy position of struggling under more than $16,000 in personal debt.

"Last year, in finance charges *alone*, you paid $759.54," Agran pointed out.

As for their assets, the Faermans had an autograph collection valued at around $1,500; a $2,000 record collection, savings bonds of $550, and stock worth around $756. Over several years, they had made a modest investment in silver bars, but had lost track of the investment's value. When silver prices plunged, they lost money.

"The majority of your investments fall into the 'risky' category," Agran said. "Entrepreneurs need to build a sound financial base of more conservative investments, such as certificates of deposit (CDs) and Treasury bills, since their primary investment—in your case, your restaurant—entails risk. To invest in things like silver, you need to be in a financial position where you won't be damaged if you lose money."

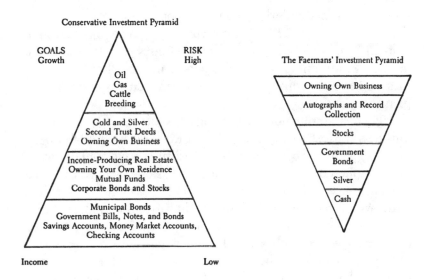

Except for the U.S. savings bonds and a CD of $1,200 owned mutually by Shari and her sister, the Faermans had no savings, owned no residence, and had established no Individual Retirement Accounts (IRAs).

"Rule number one when launching a business," Agran noted, "is that you need at least six months' savings already put away to survive on while you get the business started. You may not have realized it," she added, consulting her calculator, "but you started out with substantial debt, and that personal debt rose significantly during the year you've been in business. Consequently, it's been impossible for you to stay even, let alone save anything."

(A prudent rule for starting a new venture is to expect that it will not make a profit for at least eighteen months. Therefore, the Faermans, who were now showing a deficit of about $2,000 a month, should have had at least $36,000 more capital than they had to cushion themselves until the restaurants could work themselves into the black.)

Agran was particularly concerned about the Faermans' lack of IRAs. "They're a *must* for the entrepreneur," she counseled. "The self-employed person is very vulnerable unless he or she sets aside money on an annual basis. For people owning their own businesses, there are minimal Social Security benefits and no other pension plans."

(Agran recommended IRAs, instead of Keoghs, because a business must show a profit before a Keogh can be established.)

The Faermans' personal monthly expenses were running about $2,500 (including $600 rent and nearly $600 a month to meet the credit-card debt payments). Six months' savings to cover these costs would have totaled $15,000—ideally, money they should have put away *before* opening *Pollo Supremo*. Instead, the restaurateurs started with virtually no savings, and by the end of one year in business had accumulated $16,000 worth of personal debt and a $105,500 share of their company's business debt.

"What has happened," Agran said, "is that you have had to run one new business—which always involves a certain amount of risk—while borrowing additional money to launch another. Without any cushion to fall back on, you've tried to meet your monthly living expenses, including servicing all that personal debt, by drawing from an undercapitalized operation. No wonder you've been unable to show a profit."

"We decided we'd sell the first restaurant and concentrate on the one in Santa Paula," Gustavo said, "where our costs will be lower and our profits much more reliable. Ultimately, our goal is to start up restaurants, make them profitable, and sell within a year or two."

"Several people have been looking at the Oxnard restaurant," Shari said, "but we've had no offers yet. In the long run, the Oxnard place will make money—it's in a high-growth area, and people love the food."

When Agran asked to see the monthly financial statements detailing the income and expenses of all the business operations, the Faermans looked glum.

"We're having a problem with our accountant. He changed firms," Gustavo said.

"We chose to go with him because he specialized in restaurants," Shari explained, "but he hasn't sent us our month-end records since he moved, five months ago. I call and call, but I just don't hear back."

"This is very serious," Agran said. "With a new business, you simply *have* to have accurate and constant feedback. If anyone were seriously interested in buying the business, they'd want to take a look at the books. If they're not up-to-date, it would make them suspicious."

Agran pointed out that until the first restaurant was sold, Gustavo would be dividing his working hours between the two establishments at a time when *each* business needed an experienced full-time manager. "You've simply got to concentrate on getting your records in shape so you can sell the Oxnard place quickly and reduce your overall debt."

Agran determined the Faermans' assets and liabilities (see chart) and calculated their net worth—a shaky $7,000.

Concerned, she began to make recommendations. "Immediately, make some accurate predictions as to the costs involved in starting up the new restaurant in Santa Paula," she advised. She strongly recommended that the Faermans put the new venture, which was already under way, on a strict budget and, at the same time, put *themselves* on a strict budget.

Rule number two for entrepreneurs, she explained, is having one's personal finances under control while maintaining the business finances under the experienced and watchful eye of a first-rate accountant.

PERSONAL FINANCIAL STATEMENT

ASSETS	VALUE	OWNER	NOTES
Cash			
Savings	$ 45		
Investments:			
CDs	600	S.F.	For Baby
Bonds	550	S.F.	Savings Bonds EE
Stock	756	S.F.	
Business	90,000		
Silver	288		
Autographs	1,500		
Record collection	2,000		
Personal possessions:			
Automobiles	10,500		
Furnishings	13,000		
Clothing	2,500		
Jewelry	5,000		
Tools, equipment	150		
Parrot	2,000		
TOTAL ASSETS	$128,889		
LIABILITIES			
Current			
Charge Accounts	$ 2,064		
MasterCard	1,158		
Balance Plus	2,310		
Long-term			
Auto loan	7,591		
Education loan	3,076		
Business loan	105,500		
TOTAL LIABILITIES	$121,699		
ASSETS	$128,889		
LIABILITIES	121,699		
NET WORTH	$ 7,190		

"I suppose this would be a difficult time for us to start a family," Shari asked tentatively. "I feel an awful lot of pressure from my family. I'm twenty-nine, and my mom says she doesn't want a grandchild with feathers," she joked, nodding at Tio, who sat on his perch munching walnuts.

"Who am I to tell you about family planning," Agran replied. "But in terms of the financial aspect of having a baby—frankly, you can't afford it right now. But since you do plan to have children, I would encourage you to dedicate those $50 savings bonds Shari's grandfather sends each month to a 'Baby Fund' and let them accumulate. Just getting a baby delivered without incident costs about $3,800."

"And in terms of time," Gustavo said, "I'd never be home and you wouldn't be able to work for a year or two."

"You could consider delaying starting your family until the Oxnard restaurant is sold and the Santa Paula restaurant is profitable," Agran noted. "It would also make sense to wait until the family finances are on a sound basis. That means all personal debts paid off and at least $7,500 invested in a money market account. That's probably a delay of three or four years."

Somewhat subdued by Agran's serious tone and her austere prescription, the Faermans suggested the group adjourn to *Pollo Supremo* for lunch. It was a twenty-six-mile drive from the Faermans' apartment to the restaurant. When Agran discovered this, she had another suggestion: The Faermans should move.

"All this commuting must be very stressful," she commented when they arrived at the Oxnard restaurant. "Would you consider relocating somewhere between here and the Santa Paula restaurant, since that's where you'll eventually be spending most of your time?"

"We've been thinking about it," Shari replied, escorting everyone into the brightly lit restaurant filled with the syncopated sounds of a radio playing Mexican music. "I've felt really tired lately and my stomach's been hurting. The doctor told me my problem was that I work too much. He said seven days a week all day for a year without any time off is too much for anyone."

"It is," Agran sympathized. "If you moved, you'd save at least an hour and a half in commuting time and at least a hundred dollars a month on gas for the two cars."

It was past the luncheon hour, but business was brisk. The Faermans discussed the rising cost of food as their guests ate succulent chicken that had been marinated in tropical juices and flame-broiled. Everyone agreed: The food was delicious.

"We buy the best chicken—no preservatives, no hormones," Shari said proudly. "Our food is low in cholesterol and calories, and it's even been approved by the American Heart Association," she added, pointing to the subtly flavored beans, tortillas served with salsa, the crisp green salad, and a specialty of the house: homemade chocolate pudding blended with low-fat milk. Two pieces of chicken plus the extras came to $3.83.

"We're probably paying more for chicken than you would at the supermarket," complained Gustavo. "Even though we sell 2,000 pounds of chicken a week, we don't buy in enough volume to get a decent discount. The cost to us of everything else on the menu has gone up 10 to 20 percent in a year."

Agran urged the hardworking young couple to spend the next months concentrating on reducing their restaurant expenses by carefully monitoring where the businesses were being drained. Agran hoped the proceeds from the sale of the Oxnard restaurant would significantly reduce the balance of the $147,000 variable-interest-rate loans the Faermans had taken out when they decided to launch the second restaurant. Another loan, of $64,000 at a fixed rate, didn't concern her as much.

Agran's other recommendations included having Shari and Gustavo draw a salary from the business rather than taking partnership payments. "Continually taking partnership draws eventually reduces the value of your original investment," Agran noted. "Letting the business pay you salaries will qualify you for opening that IRA, even if the amount is small. As you head into your thirties, it's important to begin establishing a pattern for saving for your eventual retirement."

Agran asked them to spend the next few weeks examining their attitudes about spending. She urged them to pay all bills and record payments in a ledger together. "Gustavo, you're currently paying all the bills and Shari is spending the money—it's bound to create tension in a marriage. I can see you're both experiencing a great deal of anxiety. You both must share the burden and responsibility of personal and business money matters together or you won't be able to change your behavior."

In other words, Shari must feel as responsible as Gustavo does for every penny earned and spent. Toward this end, Agran asked Shari to construct a list of the couple's personal expenses for January 1 through the end of February 1984, to see where their personal money had actually been going. "Then you can *both* develop a realistic family budget."

"You want to improve your uncertain financial situation by systematically clearing up your current liabilities and keeping a close watch on personal and business expenditures," Agran continued. "Eventually, you want to be eligible for future business and real estate loans that you can qualify for."

Follow-Up

"Many times we've thought about throwing up our hands and giving up, but we're fighters," said Gustavo when *SPPFM* caught up with the busy Faermans nearly six months after the initial interview.

Their original restaurant in Oxnard had not sold as they had hoped it would. Their second restaurant, *Pollo Bravo,* was about to fling open its doors in Santa Paula, two and a half months later than originally scheduled. "After our restaurant equipment supplier went bankrupt, holding $20,000 of our money, we wondered what else could happen!"

Actually, quite a bit else had happened to the entrepreneurial Faermans in recent months. Gustavo filed complaints against the equipment supplier with local police and the district attorney, "but there's really no way for us to get our money back in the foreseeable future." Shari's father had managed to persuade a friend to loan $10,000 toward opening the new restaurant, to be paid back "as soon as we can," explained Gustavo, and another $10,000 was borrowed on a one-year loan at about 12 percent interest.

That problem was no sooner dealt with when Gustavo began having trouble with the contractor in charge of overseeing the construction of the new restaurant. "He wasn't paying some of his subcontractors, even though we'd given him the full $18,000 to do the job," Gustavo complained. "Finally, I had to fire him. We got someone to finish the work for $1,000, but that's another reason why we delayed our opening."

Another major event in the Faermans' roller-coaster existence was that Shari had an announcement: She was pregnant. "Of course, it's totally unplanned, if you remember our discussion," she noted, "but nonetheless welcome! We won't be insured for the pregnancy due to a strange coincidence of timing with the health coverage we took out last year." Shari was preparing to hold a garage sale to raise some cash, and hope to sell a new $400 TV she'd won in a contest. "Our parents and a baby shower will help."

"It's not all bad news," Gustavo hastened to add. Sales were up nearly $3,000 two months running at the Oxnard restaurant. Overhead costs will be shared soon between the two restaurants, which will help cash flow enormously.

"We've got our checkbook under control and it balances every month," Gustavo said proudly. "No more paying with money orders." The new accountant they had hired was working out beautifully. "He's really nice, reliable, and stays on top of things," he continued. "Our first-quarter statements are finally ironed out."

The Faermans reported they had stopped spending money for anything but essentials and had paid off much of their credit card debts, including most of their department store charges. All in all, the Faermans had cut $100 off their monthly expenses just by paying off those accounts. "We've even managed to put about $800 in our savings account," Gustavo added.

The Faermans are also proud of the way they now keep track of where their money goes. "We keep receipts for everything—down to 50 cents for a paper," Gustavo laughed.

The Faermans' overall business loan payments are now running about $5,000 a month. With sales up at the Oxnard restaurant, and a healthy anticipated cash flow from the Santa Paula enterprise, "I think we'll make it," says Gustavo bravely. "We're not quitters."

And Tio, the parrot? Plans are to donate him to nearby Moorpark College's exotic animal reserve for a $1,500 tax credit. His bedroom in the Faermans' apartment is reserved for their new baby.

MEET PAM WOOD AND BRUCE KIRCH

Pam Wood and Bruce Kirch represent a growing breed of American togetherness—the unmarried couple household—coded at the Census Bureau under the acronym POSSLQ or "Persons of the Opposite Sex Sharing Living Quarters."

Between 1970 and 1983, the number of POSSLQs increased by 261.6 percent. In fact, according to the Census Bureau, about 1 in 25 couples living together in 1983—or close to 2 million households—were not married.

Despite their new-fashioned living arrangements, Pam and Bruce, both in their mid-twenties, have old-fashioned financial planning needs. Like many young professional couples starting out, they have moved from the relative poverty and simple lifestyle of students to considerable affluence—without much knowledge about how to handle that affluence.

With a combined gross income of $74,000 and few major expenses, Pam and Bruce do not have financial problems, as that term is generally understood. But despite their high take-home pay, they have little idea of where their money is going, not much in the bank, and no plan for accumulating savings. They have been spending without priorities, not planning beyond the next vacation, operating on the well-known laissez-faire principle "If you've got it, spend it."

A tall, athletic couple, their lifestyle is a contemporary mixture of center-city urbanity and country sports fitness. While crazy about Boston, they are year-round athletes, devoted to skiing in winter and biking in summer. During the past year, Bruce has taken up triathlon competition, which, even as an amateur event, involves swimming several miles, biking 20–60 miles, and running 6–15 miles. Driven by their love of sports, they now share the dream of buying a house or condominium nearer to or in the country, within commuting distance of Boston.

Bruce graduated from MIT in 1981, joined General Electric in 1982, and is one year into a master's degree in manufacturing, courtesy of GE, which in general provides excellent benefits. He is now earning $32,000 as a quality control engineer for GE's Aircraft Engine Business Group and foresees a fine future with the company.

Pam, who met Bruce when she was an undergraduate at Wellesley, went to law school at the University of Pennsylvania and in 1982 joined Bingham, Dana & Gould, the large Boston law firm where she had worked summers. She is earning $42,000.

Pam and Bruce moved in together in April 1983. Since then they have functioned as separate-but-equal financial partners, with the exception of what they call "love bucks," which is basically a joint savings account. "Love bucks" pay for what they spend and use in common. The joint account was created to stop the kind of financial arguments common to people who have different spending priorities. As Pam admitted, "Within two months, after almost coming to blows at the grocery store checkout counter, we devised our system." It works particularly well because it's flexible enough for one party with an overwhelming desire for, say, a trip to New Orleans, to "buy off" the other by increasing his or her contribution to the common pot.

Nevertheless, Pam has been concerned about her lack of

knowledge and control over her finances. Money has been a problem for her since the age of fourteen, when her father died. As she put it, "For years I had to watch every penny. College and graduate school were financed through a combination of student loans, scholarships, Social Security benefits, and summer jobs. Then suddenly, I was earning all this money, but I hadn't the faintest idea what to do with it."

Pam took the first step by enrolling in a lunchtime personal budgeting seminar at the Boston Center for Adult Education.

"That was when the ledger appeared," Bruce grimly recalled several months later as he and Pam sat with financial planner Jim Sullivan in the cheerful kitchen-dining area of Pam and Bruce's $800-a-month, two-bedroom apartment in a renovated house on Boston's famed Beacon Hill.

Sullivan taught the budgeting course Pam attended, and understood where Bruce was coming from. "Most people look forward to the budget process as much as they look forward to going to the dentist," he says cheerfully. "They fear that they'll be bogged down in tracking every last nickel and dime they spend. They are concerned that they'll have to *give up* or *cut back* on their favorite pastimes—in this case traveling, vacations, and eating out. Most of all, they fear that they've been doing everything wrong."

Sullivan had given written instructions to Pam on how to develop a budget and maintain it. While he believes it's important to look at all expenditures in detail when *first* tracking and establishing a budget, "Once there's an awareness of what 'miscellaneous' is comprised of, then you only have to take a reading every six months or so, to make sure it hasn't grown exponentially."

Pam and Bruce had filled out a financial questionnaire, spent some time with Sullivan discussing their goals, and were now about to receive his counsel.

Sullivan's amiable good humor dissipated Bruce's natural reserve and remaining trace of uneasiness. Besides, he brought glad tidings. "Basically, you're in good shape. You've been relatively modest in your expenditures, which means you'll be able to achieve your goals more rapidly."

Here is what their net worth statement looked like as of June 1984:

PAM AND BRUCE'S NET WORTH AS OF JUNE 1984

ASSETS	PAM	BRUCE
Cash & Checking		
Regular Savings Account	$ 750	$ 40
Checking/NOW Accounts	700	
Certificates of Deposit	2,650	
Loans to Others		200
Total Cash	4,100	240
Liquid Investments		
Employer savings plan		6,540*
*Total of two years' deposits. Money available three years from deposit except sooner for housing or continuing education.		
Personal Property		
Auto—'83 Honda Accord Four-Door		7,000
Furniture	3,500	2,000
Clothing, Jewelry	1,500	1,000
Art, Antiques, Collectibles	600	
Total Personal Property	5,600	10,000
Retirement Plans		
Employer Pension		415
Social Security Coverage	Yes	Yes
Total Retirement Plans	0	415
TOTAL ASSETS	9,700	17,195
LIABILITIES		
Credit Card Balances	$ 2,250	$ 535
Auto Loans		5,500

ASSETS	PAM	BRUCE
Education Loans	20,418	
Other Installment Loans	300	580
TOTAL LIABILITIES	22,968	6,615
NET WORTH (assets minus liabilities)	−$13,268	$10,580

Sullivan asked Pam and Bruce to list short-term (1–12 months), intermediate (1–5 years), and long-term (more than 5 years) goals, even though he believes goals should be reviewed every nine months. Here are their goals and Sullivan's suggestions for achieving them.

Short-term goals
Through budgeting, to:

1) Become more aware of where their money is going and use their income most effectively.
2) Pay off charge accounts and get out of debt.
3) Set aside money for a major vacation each year.
4) Learn about investment options.
5) Set up an emergency cash fund and, in Pam's case, set aside money to provide "perks" for her widowed mother. (Pam recently took her mother on a cruise to Bermuda and would like to be able to continue such treats.)

Like dieters monitoring their caloric intake, Pam and Bruce found tracking their spending patterns a useful exercise. They learned that they spent less than the average couple on furniture and clothing, and more on dining out and travel. Between the time she filled in the questionnaire and she and Bruce met with Sullivan, Pam decided to cut down on the amount of money she was forking over for lunch. She resolved to brown-bag it twice a week and entertain at home more in order to save more. Bruce, too, is eager to reduce eating out so he can pay off his credit card debt. Sullivan's advice on paying off loans and credit card balances was instructive.

- Pam should use her $4,100 cash in bank accounts to pay off her $2,250 credit card balances in full. "You can see the imbalance for yourself," Sullivan pointed out. The savings can earn no more than 11½ percent in short-term CDs (only 5½ percent in regular savings accounts), while the finance-charge rates in Massachusetts are 18 percent.
- Pam's $200 a month budgeted to pay off her credit card balances should now be allocated to savings to rebuild her cash fund. In 12 months the $2,250 will be back in savings, but in the meantime she will save as much as 12½ percent in interest.
- Pam's $20,000+ education loans should *not* be paid off earlier than scheduled due to their low (average 6 percent) interest rates. Also, the interest is tax deductible (at Pam's current 42 percent tax bracket) and, even with low inflation, is being paid back in cheaper dollars.
- Bruce should pay off his credit card balance through take-home-pay budgeting.
- Bruce should *not* pay off his auto loan balance of $5,500, financed at 12 percent through GE's credit union. Instead, he should take cash earmarked to accelerate paying off that loan balance, and add it to the GE incentive savings plan—to which GE contributes. The plan *pays* 12 percent, while the loan *costs* 12 percent. The GE savings plan money will then be available for a down payment on a house.

Sullivan also suggested that Pam's concern for her mother's financial future be directed, in part, toward finding out the precise nature of her finances and, if appropriate, guiding her toward better financial and estate planning.

Intermediate goals
To buy a house or condo, prepare wills, and increase savings substantially.

The biggest surprise of the session was Sullivan's announcement that Pam and Bruce could buy a house in six months. With hardly any money in the bank, how was that possible?

Sullivan pointed out that, generally, a bank will let you devote 28 percent of your gross monthly pay to housing (mortgage, property tax, and insurance). He advised that they phone various banks and mortgage companies to obtain an approximation of what mortgage amount they would qualify for. A lower mortgage interest rate will, of course, permit a higher mortgage amount on an identical monthly payment. With an adjustable rate, Sullivan said it's important that there be an annual rate increase cap, a lifetime cap, and a rate-change index outside of the bank, such as six-month T-bills.

In general, you need 10 percent down plus about $4,000 in closing costs to purchase a house. For example, a $120,000 home will require $16,000 in cash. The amount of the mortgage you can receive plus cash available for the down payment equals the price of the house you can buy and should start looking for.

Sullivan estimated that with a mortgage rate of 13 percent for 30 years, they could support a mortgage of about $125,000 or a home of about $137,000, and would need to accumulate between $16,000 and $20,000. Bruce has accumulated $8,000 in GE's savings plan. Pam can begin socking away $200 a week, or about $800 a month, once she has paid off her credit cards. In six months, that would add up to $4,800, which would bring them in the ballpark for a mortgage of between $80,000 and $100,000. Sullivan advised them to start doing their homework—checking out mortgages, looking at houses and neighborhoods, and thinking about a second car—right away.

Here is how Sullivan estimated what Pam and Bruce could afford:

1) Combined gross monthly pay of Pam and Bruce: $3,158 + 2,656 = $5,814, or approximately $70,000 per year.
2) Multiply $5,814 × 28 percent = $1,628 for mortgage, real estate tax, insurance, etc.

3) $1,628
   - 150 month for taxes
   - 50 month for insurance
   $1,428 monthly mortgage
4) A $1,428 mortgage at 13 percent for 30 years supports a mortgage of $124,500.
5) A $124,500 mortgage plus $12,500 (10 percent down payment) = a $137,000 home (plus approximately $4,000 in closing costs).
   A more modest $80,000 mortgage plus $9,000 down would support an $89,000 home. A $9,000 down payment plus $3,500 in closing costs would require only $12,000 in cash.
6) Taxwise, $1,400 mortgage interest plus $150 real estate tax = $1,550 a month at 12 months or $18,600 in tax deductions.

Legally, unrelated people buy property together as tenants in common, and increasing numbers of couples are doing so. Each owns half the property but maintains his/her legal independence. In theory, Pam can "borrow" part of her down payment from Bruce or vice versa, and they can split the deductions evenly.

Sullivan's savings suggestions were as follows: Bruce's incentive savings plan at work is very attractive, but he has no fully liquid account for emergencies, so he should accumulate $500 as soon as possible and put it in a money market mutual fund. Pan can make better use of her savings by using a checking account for checking only, keeping the balance as low as possible, and arranging for an automatic overdraft provision so checks won't bounce. In general, 5½ percent demand deposit accounts (regular savings) should only be used for amounts less than $500. Amounts between $500 and $2,500 should go into a money market mutual fund; over $2,500 should go into a bank money market account. While liquidity is important when thinking about a home purchase, Pam and Bruce should think about six-month CDs as a savings vehicle, if yields are attractive. (Any unexpected income, like tax refunds, should be put into savings without thinking twice.)

He advised against IRAs for both Bruce and Pam until after they had purchased a home. "Right now," Sullivan said, "the GE savings plan looks better, and if you're going to invest your savings in a home fairly quickly, it makes little sense to put your money in an IRA, where you're penalized for withdrawing funds."

The financial and legal considerations of unmarried household couples can get very tangled. The issue of drawing up wills made that clear.

"To begin with, wills are a necessity if you want possessions or benefits to pass to the person you are living with [other than items that are jointly owned with right of survivorship, in writing]," Sullivan said. "Without a will, property will go to *any* relative first and, if there are no relatives, to the state."

Therefore, Sullivan deemed wills for Pam and Bruce an absolute must. He further pointed out that unmarrieds don't qualify for pension joint or survivor benefits, but can be named as pension beneficiaries.

Since Pam and Bruce have relatively few assets and Pam works at a law firm, it was estimated that wills could be professionally prepared for about $75 each.

Sullivan also urged Bruce to get renter's insurance, since Pam's coverage does not extend to his property or liability. That means that if *his* Italian racing bike were stolen from *their* apartment, for example, he would not be covered by *her* renter's insurance. He also believed they should consider obtaining excess personal liability coverage.

Both have excellent disability and medical insurance through their employers.

Long-term goals

As for their long-term goal of owning rental property, Sullivan encouraged them, given their sports lifestyle, to investigate vacation rental property after they purchased a home.

Pam and Bruce were anxious to start implementing their plans. They intended to begin right after a week's vacation at the Olympics in Los Angeles, where Bruce's sister competed as a member of the U.S. women's crew team.

Follow-Up

Two months after their meeting with Sullivan, Pam and Bruce had implemented most of their goals and had a clear time frame for when they would carry out the rest of their plan.

Bruce had tracked his significant expenses, set up a budget, paid off his charge accounts, and purchased renter's insurance, as well as supplementary car and personal liability insurance. He is pleased with his ability to better plan and control his expenditures and has modified his spending patterns. There are fewer spur-of-the-moment meals out or impulsive purchases. For example, Bruce and Pam are setting aside $10 a month to buy a tape deck rather than just going out and buying one.

Basically, Bruce feels his eyes have been opened to such basic principles as where tax savings come from and how to optimize income. He is reading more literature on the subject of real estate investments.

Pam seems to be equally delighted by her increased knowledge of financial matters. She proudly related how, when a stockbroker tried to persuade her to invest in his company's money market fund, she pointed out to him that her bank's rates were better and not taxed, as his would be, as an out-of-state investment. "He was really impressed," she reports.

Pamela has paid off her charge accounts, opened a checking account with overdraft privileges as well as a bank money market fund. She is diligently saving money for vacations, including a Seoul fund for the '88 Olympics, where Bruce's sister again wants to compete, and is brown-bagging it at work about 50 percent of the time. In addition to setting aside money for "extras" for her mom, she has begun investigating ways for her mother to transfer her major real estate assets to her children now.

Both Pam and Bruce have drawn up wills. However, despite their ability to purchase a home this year, they have decided to renew the lease on their apartment and begin the process of looking for a house or condo next spring. High interest rates were a factor in their decision, but in addition, the couple recognized they were not yet psychologically ready to devote the time and energy required of the task. As Bruce put it, "There's no rush, and this way we can save for a down payment without an austerity budget in other parts of our lives."

MEET LISA ROBINSON AND KIM TREVIRANUS

They have ordered the matching rings, the dress, and the invitations, met the minister, selected flowers, and arranged for an elegant brunch for sixty-five friends in a private room at a favorite restaurant.

Lisa A. Robinson, twenty-seven, a pharmacist at the University of Illinois Department of Dermatology, and Kim Treviranus, a thirty-two-year-old internal medicine resident and pulmonary fellow at the University of Illinois Hospital, are getting married in four weeks.

"At this moment, we're calm," Lisa says. "Kim and I just walk around with our lists, checking things off. Now all we have to do is sit here and wait for everything to go wrong!"

Like many young, career-oriented professionals, Lisa and Kim are highly organized. The couple has worked out all the details of their wedding day, the two-week honeymoon sailing off the island of Maui, Hawaii, and the complicated move from two apartments in two different Chicago suburbs to a first home in Dixon, Ill., several hours away.

And, in the past few weeks, they have made several key decisions about their futures. Kim will begin his medical career as one of six salaried internists in a ten-year-old medical clinic, and Lisa will take the summer off—her first in nine years—to refinish furniture and do other chores around the three-bedroom, two-bath house they've just purchased. In September, she will enter law school to prepare for a new career combining law and health.

While Lisa and Kim have planned their immediate future with great care, their long-term goals are less specific. "We eventually will have kids—probably two," says Lisa, "but I'd like to wait until I've finished law school. And Kim's been putting together plans for the dream house we plan to build somewhere down the road."

Kim is pensive as he speaks of the future. "I don't want to work all my life. I want to travel and do things," he explains. "When I started medical school eight years ago, they told us the average life expectancy for a doctor was fifty-eight. This is crazy, I thought. I want to save enough money so that I can begin to take life a little easier when I'm fifty-five." He looks at Lisa. "And I'd also like to have enough money put aside so that if anything *should* happen to me, there'd be enough for Lisa to live on until she finished school or found a ready source of income doing something she really wanted to do."

With these weighty matters in mind, and a 50-page personal financial planning case analysis in hand (a document they had filled out in preparation for their meeting with certified financial planner Mike Leonetti) they approached Leonetti's Arlington Heights, Illinois, offices to begin mapping out their financial future.

"We're here to talk about what we'd like to do with our money, and the truth is that right now we don't have any," says Lisa by way of introduction. (The couple's net worth works out to $9,731.)

"Medical school and the medical profession, when you're just beginning, is a study in poverty," Kim explains. "It's all debt and loans, payments and catch-up." Yet Kim and Lisa were able to buy a house with 100 percent financing. "It's incredible," says Kim, "but the banks out there are fighting one another for doctors' business."

Despite $11,000 worth of student loans and the mortgage on their house, the couple is hardly in dangerous—or even turbulent—financial waters. As single professionals, each earning around $30,000 a year (Kim moonlighted in the emergency room of the University of Illinois Hospital while in medical school), Lisa and Kim have been sensible, practical money managers. They have each financed and paid off a car, furnished a one-bedroom apartment, and generally lived within their incomes. They've even been able to contribute to the support of young children in other countries.

"The fact that, in Dixon, we were able to buy a great house for $64,000 that would have cost at least $150,000 anywhere else has really helped," says Lisa. "Our $635 monthly payments for the house are actually less than the combined rents for our two apartments. I'm not planning any peanut butter sandwich/ Campbell soup dinners for the next few years because I think we're in a very reasonable situation—we're not over our heads at all, even with the loans.

"But there is something that scares me." Lisa leans forward. "Kim and I are getting married and suddenly we're going into a situation where we're almost doubling our income because Kim alone is going to be making almost $100,000 a year." She shakes her head. "We're going to be making all this money and there'll be all those taxes to pay, and we have no way to shelter our money."

The future tax bite

"You're right to be concerned," Leonetti begins, turning to the questionnaire Lisa and Kim completed. Leonetti's copy had been run through a computer program to test out different tax and investment strategies.

"Like many young doctors, you're suddenly going to have a high income—an income tax bracket of about 40 percent this year, and at least 45 percent or more next year—and a lot of debt to pay off.

"As far as tax relief goes, you're in a temporary Catch-22 situation," Leonetti points out, "because if you go into a tax shelter plan now, you won't have any money for emergencies. If the clinic Kim is working with has a qualified retirement plan, you can shelter some dollars there. But if it doesn't, you may have to explore incorporation as a means of reducing taxes. But that is something that can be looked at next year, when you have everything else in place.

"Your immediate objective is to build up an emergency cash fund. You need to accumulate assets and keep your money liquid."

Emergency funds

"Watch where your money is going and get into the habit of saving," Leonetti counsels. "You've been living close to your incomes, but you should continue to be realistic about what you can afford to spend and what you should put away. *Treat yourself as a top priority bill on your list of expenses and pay yourself savings first, before the mortgage or your electric bill.* You don't have to decide at this very minute just exactly how much you are going to save. In fact, you should wait until you get into your home and see how it all comes together. But start building up your cash reserves and establish an emergency fund now.

"I suggest you aim for $8,000, and put that into a tax-free money market fund like T. Rowe Price. In your tax bracket, you'd be realizing an after-tax return of about 12 percent on your money. Then, when you've reached your $8,000 goal, it'll be possible to reposition those dollars."

Expenses

"To mèet your savings target and other financial goals, your household and family expenses must be watched very carefully, because that's where the dollars disappear," Leonetti cautions.

Because Lisa and Kim are just beginning their married life, they have had no experience yet with a combined budget, so Leonetti has encouraged them to "guesstimate" what they will be spending in the various categories.

Lisa's estimates of $100 for utilities, $50 for telephone, $100 for auto maintenance and gas, and $300 for home maintenance may prove to be totally unrealistic, "but at least she has started thinking about the " Leonetti emphasizes.

The amount of oney Lisa and Kim have budgeted to spend

on their new home is minimal because the house is basically in good shape.

"We won't need to buy some of the basics because we have two of almost everything," Lisa says. "Two toasters, blenders, and irons—even two vacuum cleaners. I've been on my own for nine years and Kim for fourteen, so we've accumulated a lot of things."

Although Lisa and Kim are not splurge-spenders, they do share one extravagance. They plan an annual out-of-the-ordinary vacation costing several thousand dollars. "We like to see new places and do things we've never done before," Kim explains. "We both work out regularly, and when we go on vacation, we take guided trips like trekking or backpacking in some out-of-the-way place, or we go bicycling in Vermont or snorkeling. Sometimes these kinds of vacations end up being expensive because we buy all the equipment and gear. I guess if we really needed to save money, we could cut out our vacations.

"I'm not the kind of person who's interested in amassing a great deal of wealth and then leaving it to someone else," says Kim. "Money is nice, but lifestyle is better." This philosophy guided Kim in his choice of a post-residency job. He chose a salaried clinic position with regular working hours over a position in private practice, where he could have earned twice as much money but would be working day and night.

Lisa's attitude about money is a little less disciplined. "I always feel I should be saving money but I still spend it," she confesses. She doesn't follow a formal budget because "all budgets are kind of flexible anyway and I really feel that making the right choices is what budgeting is all about anyway."

"How much you spend and on what is relative to your particular lifestyle," Leonetti says. "But putting down what you spend and getting a handle on your money shows you just where you are. Then, if you need more dollars in one area, you know you have to spend less in another area, and you can see immediately where you have to cut back."

One area where cutbacks should not be made is insurance.

As newlyweds, with considerable financial obligations, Kim and Lisa should explore their insurance needs carefully, Leonetti urges.

Insuring a new lifestyle
Kim has a $15,000 life insurance policy, which Leonetti recommends he cancel. "Take the $2,000 cash value from that policy, put the money in your money fund, and then purchase a new $135,000 term insurance policy. The premiums for the new policy will end up costing you $52 a year less than what you now pay and you'll have more coverage."

Kim and Lisa will be entitled to medical care through the clinic where Kim works, and Leonetti says the clinic policy is a particularly good one. He checks off all the pluses: an 80/20 co-insurance with a $5,000 stop-loss clause, which means that the most Kim or Lisa would have to pay out-of-pocket for medical expenses in any one year is $1,000; 100 percent coverage of hospital costs; and 100 percent coverage for maternity; which, under the terms of this policy, is treated as an illness.

The new homeowners policy for the Dixon house also provides good coverage. It has an inflation guard, comprehensive liability, and, in case of total loss, provides for full replacement. The move to Dixon has resulted in another saving. Lisa reports that the insurance premiums for both their autos in Dixon are less than she was paying previously to insure her car alone!

Leonetti suggests that even though they now have $300,000 liability coverage on their homeowners insurance, they may want to consider adding a million-dollar umbrella policy. "It only costs about $100 a year, but it will protect you against any large lawsuits, and you may consider it necessary as your assets grow. Because doctors are highly visible persons in any community, it's assumed that all doctors have money—even when they're just beginning.

"As a matter of fact, an umbrella policy is a good thing to have even if you're not a doctor," Leonetti adds. "If someone slips on your sidewalk or you have an accident, you could be open to all kinds of claims. And speaking of claims, how will you be covered for malpractice suits?" Leonetti asks Kim.

"I hope to get coverage through my clinic's plan. As an internist, my insurance costs are among the lowest in the profession."

"Disability insurance is something you're not covered for by the clinic," Leonetti observes, "and it's important that you protect yourself and Lisa if you do become disabled and are unable to produce an income. Because there's so much confusion in this area, disability insurance is hard to shop for."

Leonetti explained that the first and most important thing in shopping for disability insurance is checking the policy's definition of disability. "A good definition is an inability to perform the normal duties of your occupation. Some companies write very good disability policies for physicians.

"I recommend that you present all your insurance needs at the same time to the company and then get competitive bids for the plan that's right for you. It will cost you a lot less time.

"Another way to save on disability premiums is to request a policy with a 90-day waiting period. This could almost halve your premium. Don't sign for any policy unless you know exactly what the rates will be," Leonetti cautions. "A good agent should be able to give you a rate schedule for the next 20 years."

Immediate concerns
Lisa has a very immediate question. She will receive almost $8,000 in retirement funds when she leaves her job at the University of Illinois. She's been thinking of using the money to buy a new car or to pay for her tuition at Northern Illinois University, which she figures will be about $2,000 a year. Leonetti points out that she can save paying taxes on that $8,000 by putting it into an IRA rollover plan.

The IRS allows pension funds to be rolled over, without tax penalty, into a recognized IRA plan, he explains. "In an emergency, you can always pull that money out. And there's an extra advantage in your tax bracket. In six years, the tax advantages of having that original $8,000 plus compounded interest in an IRA account will more than offset any penalties you may incur for withdrawing early. *People shouldn't think of IRAs as long-term or locked-in funds.* They're part of your assets."

Another asset the couple has almost ignored is the $550 Kim has invested with his stock investment club. "There are two ways to look at this $550," Leonetti concedes. "We can say that here we are trying to create a sound, conservative investment base and there's $550 floating around that could be earning interest. Or we could shrug our shoulders and say, well, it's only $550 and these guys are good friends of mine and I don't want to hurt anyone's feelings by pulling it out."

"Well, it is a way of keeping up with my friends," Kim answers. "And I really think of it more as a hobby and a way to get some experience in what I'm supposed to be doing with money when I get some. There are twelve of us in this—a few accountants, dentists, and someone in advertising. We get all the magazines and newsletters from the National Association of Investment Clubs and we talk things over."

Lisa has been sitting quietly, listening. "What about our income tax situation for *this* year? Will we have to pay more or are we pretty well evened out?"

Leonetti is reassuring. "With all your withholding and your double payment of taxes on the house to cover last year's unpaid taxes, you won't be too far off between what was withheld and what is due. And income averaging should help, too."

He turns to Kim. "I know you're not comfortable with your student loans, but I think you should leave them out there and pay them back as scheduled. Those preferential interest rates are very favorable and you can deduct the interest on your taxes."

"I've also been thinking of working one day a week either at a pharmacy or maybe even teaching a jazz class," Lisa volunteers. "The most I'll probably earn will be $6,000. Will that create more tax problems? I've been exercising for the last four years and I'd really hate to give that up. I want to keep in shape and I don't think there's a studio or class in Dixon.

"And there's another reason. I've been on my own for so long that the thought of asking Kim for money is driving me crazy. How can I ask him for money so that I can go out and buy him presents?"

"Well, it might well mean that you'll have to pay a little more in taxes," Leonetti agrees, "but that shouldn't be a factor in your decision." He suggests that Lisa and Kim might want to discuss how they want to handle their finances and whether they want to have joint or individual accounts.

"What about the down payment bank loan hanging over our heads?" Lisa asks. "I'm not sure why I'm uncomfortable with that. I'd like to get that taken care of real quickly."

Kim explains the financing of their new home. Essentially, 90 percent of the $64,000 is a three-year balloon loan at 12 percent and the other 10 percent is financed on a six-month adjustable loan. "We're now paying 13 percent on that. We pay as much as we can, whenever we can, on that one. And we're not penalized for paying as fast as we're able to."

"Can you get a 13 percent cap on that loan?" Leonetti asks.

Kim says no. "What they basically told us at the bank is they would try to hold the rate at whatever it is for a short-term loan. And if we pay it right away, there's no difficulty renewing it."

"Well, you could make paying off the smaller loan one of your first priorities then," Leonetti comments.

"Sometime during the next few years, as your assets rise in value, you may want to rethink the joint ownership of your home. For a physician just starting out, 90–95 percent of assets held in joint tenancy is fairly common. In your case, this would be your home. In a conservative, balanced financial plan, real estate would tend to run about 35–40 percent of your net worth. Another 35–40 percent would be in a qualified retirement plan, and the remainder of the assets could be split up between different accounts such as savings, stocks, money markets, etc.

"As you begin to accumulate some dollars, you'll be in a position to consider other investments," Leonetti notes. "Building a strong financial plan is like building a pyramid. You start with a strong base, safe liquid investments, and good insurance coverage, and then you move up the ladder. And eventually, when you build up your estate and begin to have children, you'll want to draw up a will."

"It sounds impressive," Kim sums up, "and like a lot of things in life, not really as overwhelming as I thought it would be. At least we're on our way and we're in charge."

Follow-Up

"It looks like the best way to save money is to become too busy to spend it," Kim comments three months after the couple's wedding.

"We've actually been able to put away a significant amount of cash—$1,500 to be exact," Kim states with pride, "and we're hoping to bring that amount up to $5,000 by December."

"The new guy on the block," Kim puts in a long, full day at the clinic and, when he gets home in the evening, studies for his pulmonary boards. Lisa, who commutes forty-five minutes each way to Northern Illinois University School of Law, spends an additional five to six hours in study each night.

"We've become very boring people, I'm afraid," Lisa says. "School is more work than I imagined, and we'll be spending the next three years doing this. We just don't have time to spend money now on anything but food.

"I thought we'd be able to start saving money with Kim's first paycheck in July, but we had a lot of bills to pay when we got back from our honeymoon."

The wedding costs were more than Lisa and Kim had budgeted because they neglected to figure in flowers for everybody and the cost of the hotel rooms they'd provided for out-of-town guests. And even though they had decided not to have a professional photographer, the cost of making prints from color slides taken by friends ended up being more expensive than they'd anticipated.

Lisa and Kim have decided to pay Lisa's $2,000 yearly tuition and the $500 book fee out of current income. And they will defer paying off the short-term loan for another six months and pay the interest charges only when that note comes due. "It seems sensible," notes Lisa, "and the interest is deductible on our taxes."

The couple reports that household expenses seem to be in line with their expectations so far, although they are concerned about the winter heating bills because the house has no storm windows. They've ordered a $15 energy audit from the local gas company to determine the cheapest and most effective way to save on heating.

They're also apprehensive about Lisa's car, which has recently had problems.

"I think we're going to trade in one of the wrecks," Lisa says, "and buy a four-wheel drive for between $10,000 and $14,000. People say the winters out here in this open country are pretty rough, and we both have to be able to get out in bad weather. We've been talking about financing."

Kim has also been talking with the other clinic doctors about incorporating, and he has an appointment to discuss the possibility with an accountant. The clinic has initiated a new disability insurance plan, which he plans to check out.

"I feel bad because we haven't done everything Mike said we should," Lisa adds. "It's just really hard to pay yourself first before you pay the bills. I think it's going to take us about six months to get things going and get our budget working so that we can save regularly. That'll make us both feel more comfortable."

CONCLUSION

ou have now read about some of the significant ways in which love and money affect each other, whatever lifestyle you choose and whatever your romantic situation is. The vital factors that will help you get the most out of both your love life and your financial life are:

- **Communicate.** This is the key to all healthy financial relationships. Across the board, communication is the single most important element in harmonious cooperation on money matters. Without open discussion, small differences over the handling of finances soon can turn into major problems. But seemingly irreconcilable differences can usually be whittled down to manageable size when all the sides to the story are aired.

- **Examine the issues.** It's a fact of life, of course, that knowing the right question will assist you in defining your answer. Before you can truly talk or plan or make any decision about love or money, you need to be sure of the facts. However tempted you may be to look the other way, don't. What do you actually want? How do you really feel? What long-term or short-term objectives are you seeking? Where do you agree, or disagree, with your partner? A course of action that does not take all factors into account is actually a collision course with disaster.
- **Keep informed.** The world of finance is constantly changing, and you owe it to yourself to keep alert. As tax rules change, you may discover ways of saving you and your partner many tax dollars. As your circumstances change, you may want to adopt approaches to handling your finances that weren't appropriate before. Check out all the options. It makes sense to make an effort, because the cost of ignorance can be very high.
- **Plan ahead.** Do you have a financial plan? It's possible to get by without one, but it isn't smart. Part of living life to the fullest is setting goals and then achieving them. And since the future is uncertain, it also makes sense to protect yourself against any setbacks that may lie ahead. A good financial plan takes care of you: It allows you to live well right now, it enables you to make the most of your life's opportunities, and it provides a safety net when you need one. It also keeps pace with the relationships in your life as they come and go. Take the time to reassess your financial plan whenever a serious emotional commitment is made or broken.
- **Be realistic.** However euphoric or despairing your romantic affairs may make you feel, it pays to be practical with your wallet. An impartial prenuptial agreement, for example, could turn out to be unnecessary or it could save you thousands of dollars. An objective look at the spending habits of your beloved, however enchanting he or she may be, could save your credit rating. When money is mixed up with strong emo-

tions—not just devotion, but guilt, for example, or rage—the results can be unfortunate.

When you are clear-eyed about the finances of your relationships, you can only benefit from this knowledge. If this book has helped you define how love and money interact in your life, then it has served its purpose.

INDEX